GI meals
made easy

First published in 2006 by New Holland Publishers (UK) Ltd
London • Cape Town • Sydney • Auckland

Garfield House
86–88 Edgware Road
London W2 2EA
www.newhollandpublishers.com

80 McKenzie Street
Cape Town 8001
South Africa

Level 1, Unit 4
14 Aquatic Drive
Frenchs Forest, NSW 2086
Australia

218 Lake Road
Northcote
Auckland
New Zealand

1 3 5 7 9 10 8 6 4 2

ISBN 1 84537 489 4

Senior Editor: Corinne Masciocchi
Design: Sue Rose
Jacket photography: Stuart West
Editorial Direction: Rosemary Wilkinson
Production: Hazel Kirkman

Reproduction by Modern Age Repro, Hong Kong
Printed and bound by Star Standard Industries, Singapore

GI meals
made easy

Dr Barbara Wilson

NEW
HOLLAND

contents

Low GI cookery: the basics

If you have ever been on a diet, you might expect a recipe book of health-conscious meals to be full of rules on what you can't have. This isn't that book!

The recipes in this book do follow the principles of GI but these are certainly not meals that will make you feel as if you're being punished for eating healthily! You won't need to make one meal for you and another meal for the rest of the family and these recipes can be used for everyday dinners as well as for entertaining.

There are suggestions for breakfasts to help you start your day the low GI way, packed lunches, salads and side dishes, and even desserts. Yes, desserts can be healthy, nutritious and low GI!

What is GI?

So what is GI all about? The glycaemic index was originally conceived as a way to help those with diabetes control their condition. GI is a method of ranking carbohydrate foods based on the impact they have on blood glucose and insulin levels.

When we eat carbohydrate foods, these are eventually broken down to the simple sugar glucose. This glucose enters the bloodstream and from there, will either be taken to wherever the body requires energy or will be stored as fat in cells called adipose tissue. The hormone insulin is responsible for taking extra glucose out of circulation and storing it away to provide energy another time. If our energy intake exceeds our energy use, we gain weight. If our energy expenditure exceeds intake, then we use those fat cells as our energy source and we lose weight.

So, back to GI. GI values are measured by comparing foods with glucose. When glucose is eaten, it rapidly makes its way into the bloodstream and that prompts the release of insulin which then stores away extra glucose. What we experience is a sudden surge in blood sugars followed by an equally sudden drop as insulin carries out its job. So glucose is used as the reference food against which all other foods are compared. White bread could also be used as a reference food since this is also broken down rapidly and causes a substantial glycaemic response, but glucose is the more commonly used standard.

High GI foods are those that cause blood sugar levels to rise quickly and prompt a surge in insulin. In practice, this means that we feel an energy rush as the sugar hits our blood stream, followed by a low as insulin causes that sugar to be stored away. High GI values are those of 70 and above.

Medium GI foods do not have such a marked impact on blood sugars or insulin and medium GI values are categorized as being between 56 and 69.

Low GI foods are those that have little impact on blood glucose and insulin levels. Instead of causing peaks and troughs, low GI foods cause a very gradual and steady rise in glucose and insulin levels. In practice, this means that we won't feel the energy highs and lows associated with eating high GI foods and our energy levels remain more stable.

How does GI help us make healthier choices?

Following the principles of low GI eating can help us make healthier food choices and help us manage our weight. Insulin, the hormone secreted in response to increases in blood glucose, also stimulates appetite. If we avoid over-stimulating the production of insulin, then we can help avoid food cravings.

Low GI foods also tend to be higher in dietary fibre and this is what makes foods bulky and slower to digest. So, eating low GI foods can help us feel fuller for longer, making it easier for us to eat less if we're trying to lose weight.

Eating mostly low GI foods also means that we prompt insulin less often and less intensely. Our bodies can become desensitized to insulin: we need to produce more and more insulin for it to carry out its role effectively. This can lead to the development of type 2 diabetes (type 1 occurs when our bodies simply cannot make insulin). So low GI eating can help protect against type 2 diabetes.

Another benefit of following a low GI diet is protection against heart disease. Fat storage around the abdomen or trunk, as promoted by the action of insulin, increases our risk for heart disease. If we decrease the amount of insulin we produce by avoiding high GI foods, we avoid gaining excess weight around our tummies and reduce this risk factor.

A newly recognized condition, metabolic syndrome, can also be managed through low GI eating. One characteristic of this condition is carrying excess weight around the trunk and since a low GI diet helps minimize abdominal obesity, it can lower the risk of developing the condition which is thought to be a risk factor for diabetes and heart disease.

GI as part of a healthy diet

It's important not to think of GI in isolation – traditional healthy eating guidelines still apply! A balanced diet looks like the healthy eating plate. This is an easy way to tell if your meals follow healthy eating principles.

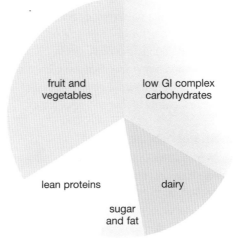

fruit and vegetables

low GI complex carbohydrates

lean proteins

dairy

sugar and fat

The main points to bear in mind are:
- one third of your plate should be made up of fruit and vegetables
- another third should be low GI complex carbohydrates
- the final third should be split between lean proteins, dairy products and sources of sugar and fat

We've mentioned that GI measures the impact of carbohydrates on the body so this means that fat and protein foods cannot really have their GI values tested. When a food contains a lot of fat or protein as well as carbohydrate, this can actually lower the GI value of that food. So a high fat – and high calorie – food can have a low GI value.

If you look at GI food tables, you might be surprised by some of the categorizations. Sponge cake, ice cream, chocolate nut

7

spread and chocolate are all low or medium GI foods. This, unfortunately, doesn't make them healthy food choices on a day-to-day basis. It does mean that we can include these occasionally but for best nutrition, we really want to focus on foods that have low GI values, relatively low fat content and provide vitamins, minerals and other nutrients. In practical terms, choose wholegrain bread (medium GI, low fat) over white bread (high GI, low fat), grilled chicken (low saturated fat, low GI) instead of minced beef (higher saturated fat, low GI) and, of course, eat plenty of fruit and vegetables.

About the recipes

Each recipe has a key, showing preparation time and cooking time as well as the following information on suitability for different diets:

$\mathcal{V}$ = suitable for vegetarians

✕ = gluten free

✕ = dairy free

= source of fibre. The recipe is particularly rich in dietary fibre, useful for giving a feeling of satiety (fullness) and important for a healthy digestive system

♥ = heart healthy. The recipe contains foods that contain essential fatty acids, which can help balance cholesterol levels

= counts towards 5-a-day. A serving will provide a fruit or vegetable portion, helping you reach your target of 5 per day

✕ = lower fat. The recipe is especially low in total and saturated fat

Many of the recipes given can be modified to suit those with dietary restrictions. For instance, those with coeliac disease, an intolerance to the protein gluten which is found primarily in wheat and cereal-based products, will need to use gluten-free staples, such as gluten-free flour (rice, corn, soya, tapioca, gram, potato and buckwheat flour are all gluten free), gluten-free bread and gluten-free oats. Other foods which often have 'hidden' gluten include yoghurt, porridge, muesli, sausages, burgers, stock, curry powder, soy sauce, ketchup, stuffing, gravy granules and baking powder.

Anyone wishing to avoid dairy products can replace milk with soy, rice or almond milk and substitute yoghurt or crème fraîche with soy yoghurt.

Menu master

Many of the recipes in this book complement each other in style and flavour and work well as full menus or dinner party dishes. Here are some suggestions:

MEZZE PLATTER

Hummus *(p 54)*
Carrot and fennel salad *(p 68)*
Roast pepper and walnut dip *(p 35)*
Butter bean and chorizo salad *(p 65)*
Italian-style meatballs with tomato sauce *(p 114)*
Marinated olives *(p 58)*
Spiced pitta chips *(p 69)*

SPRING DINNER PARTY

Fresh mint and pea soup *(p 46)*
Parma-wrapped monkfish *(p 137)*
Mixed green vegetables with crème fraîche *(p 153)*
Apricots with mascarpone cream *(p 163)*

8

SUMMER DINNER PARTY
Chicken liver pâté *(p 29)*
Cajun salmon *(p 131)*
Orange and coriander barley salad *(p 59)*
Strawberries with citrus
  mascarpone *(p 165)*

AUTUMN DINNER PARTY
Celeriac remoulade *(p 146)*
Braised pork chops with apples *(p 113)*
Baby vegetables en papillotte *(p 151)*
Individual rhubarb crumbles *(p 160)*

WINTER DINNER PARTY
Rocket and goat's cheese soup *(p 47)*
Rib-eye steaks with butter bean and
  horseradish mash *(p 101)*
Roast butternut squash *(p 152)*
Poached nectarines *(p 167)*

ASIAN-INSPIRED MEAL
Thai chicken skewers *(p 127)*
Sea bass with Asian spices *(p 134)*
Quick vegetable satay *(p 83)*
Cardamom-scented mango *(p 171)*

MEDITERRANEAN FEAST
Marinated olives *(p 58)*
Cannellini bean salad *(p 57)*
Lamb with preserved lemon bulgar *(p 109)*
Roast artichokes and tomatoes
  with feta *(p 84)*
Apricots and mascarpone cream *(p 163)*

INDIAN MEAL
Dhal *(p 157)*
Fish curry *(p 135)*
Indian-style vegetables *(p 148)*
Bombay potatoes *(p 145)*

BBQ
Smoked mackerel and cucumber
  salad *(p 140)*
Turkey with soy, honey and mustard
  (p 122)
Steak sandwich with tomatoes
  and horseradish *(p 106)*
Lime, coconut and sesame kebabs *(p 123)*
Balsamic mushrooms *(p 150)*
New potatoes with yoghurt and
  caper dressing *(p 149)*

PICNIC
Spicy bean pâté *(p 31)*
Red pesto cream cheese dip *(p 33)*
Rye bread *(p 16)*
Garlic, onion and chive tart *(p 82)*
Crab, cucumber and watercress
  pittas *(p 66)*
Flapjacks *(p 23)*

9

Healthy eating really can be easy and tasty. If you're pushed for time, make the most of prepared vegetables and salads in the supermarket and look for the recipes in this book with the shortest preparation and cooking times. If you're on a budget, buy dried beans instead of tinned and prepare veggies from scratch. Whatever your situation, fit healthy, low GI eating into your life. It's worth it!

breakfast

1

Banana milkshake smoothie

Smoothies are a great way to get fruit and dairy portions in one easy step. They don't take long to make, but make it easier on yourself in the morning, especially if you're in a rush, by getting the blender out of the cupboard and the ingredients measured out the previous evening.

PREPARATION TIME: less than 10 minutes
COOKING TIME: none
SERVES 2

1 banana
100 ml (3½ fl oz) low-fat yoghurt
100 ml (3½ fl oz) ice cold semi-skimmed milk
30 g (1 oz) jumbo oat flakes
Good pinch of cinnamon

Place all the ingredients in a blender and whiz until smooth.

Triple fruit smoothie

Fruit juice only counts once per day towards your daily target of five portions of fruit and vegetables. That's because juicing fruit removes its valuable fibre and makes the sugars more easily available, but the inclusion here of banana and strawberries (or any other fruit you enjoy) means each serving counts as two fruit portions.

PREPARATION TIME: less than 10 minutes
COOKING TIME: none
SERVES 2

1 banana
150 g (5½ oz) strawberries
200 ml (7 fl oz) orange juice

Place all the ingredients in a blender and whiz until smooth.

$\mathcal{V}$ = suitable for vegetarians   X = gluten free   X = dairy free   = source of fibre

Mango and coconut smoothie

This smoothie calls for very ripe mango – if your mango is slightly under-ripe, the smoothie could have a gritty texture. So if you'd prefer a smoother smoothie, boil the under-ripe fruit pieces in the coconut milk for five minutes. Cool before making the smoothie.

PREPARATION TIME: less than 10 minutes

COOKING TIME: none

SERVES 2

½ ripe mango
100 ml (3½ fl oz) reduced-fat coconut milk
100 ml (3½ fl oz) semi-skimmed milk
100 ml (3½ fl oz) low-fat natural or fruit yoghurt
½ lime

13

1 Cut the mango almost in half lengthways, cutting as close to the stone as possible. Then make diagonal slits across the mango flesh so the flesh is cut into diamonds – this allows you to simply cut the mango diamonds from the skin.

2 Transfer the mango, coconut milk, milk and yoghurt into a blender along with the zest from the lime. Blitz until smooth and season with lime juice.

 = heart healthy   = counts towards 5-a-day   = lower fat

Fig and pecan yeast bread

This bread can also be made in a bread machine, if you have one. Add the ingredients and follow the manufacturer's guidelines as machines vary, using a sachet of instant yeast instead of dried yeast. Follow the programme for hot cross buns.

PREPARATION TIME: less than 30 minutes + proving time
COOKING TIME: 30–60 minutes
MAKES 1 loaf

260 ml (9½ fl oz) lukewarm water
½ tsp granulated sugar
2 tsp dried yeast
400 g (14 oz) wholemeal flour
1 scant tsp salt
100 g (3½ oz) dried figs, chopped
50 g (2 oz) pecan nuts, chopped
1 Tbsp melted butter

1 Pour the water into a jug (the water needs to be around body temperature), add the sugar, stir, and sprinkle over the dried yeast. Set aside for around 10 minutes to sponge, that is, until a beery head forms.

2 Place the flour and salt into a large bowl and stir in the chopped figs and pecan nuts. Make a well in the centre and pour in the sponged yeast along with the melted butter. Stir with a wooden spoon to combine – the dough should be moist and firm but not sticky.

3 Place the dough on a floured work surface and knead gently for about five minutes, until the dough becomes smooth. Place in a large bowl and either set somewhere warm for around two hours, or place in the fridge overnight. The dough will double in volume.

4 After this time, preheat the oven to 220° C (425° F/gas mark 7) and line a 2-lb loaf tin with baking parchment. Give the dough another light knead, just for a couple of minutes, then place in the tin. Bake in the preheated oven for 10 minutes, then lower the heat to 190° C (375° F/gas mark 5) and bake for a further 30–40 minutes, until the bread sounds hollow when tapped on the bottom. Remove from the tin and leave to cool on a wire rack.

$\mathcal{V}$ = suitable for vegetarians   ✗ = gluten free   ✗ = dairy free   = source of fibre

Prune and walnut bread

This is a bread similar to a wheaten bread in that it doesn't require yeast. So it's quick to make and doesn't need kneading or proving time.

PREPARATION TIME: less than 30 minutes

COOKING TIME: 30–60 minutes

MAKES 1 loaf

300 g (10½ oz) wholemeal flour
125 g (4½ oz) plain flour
½ tsp cream of tartar
½ tsp baking soda
½ tsp salt
50 g (2 oz) caster sugar
100 g (3½ oz) prunes, chopped
50 g (2 oz) walnuts, chopped
50 g (2 oz) margarine, melted
300 ml (10½ fl oz) semi-skimmed milk
1 egg

1 Line a 2-lb loaf tin with baking parchment and preheat the oven to 180° C (350° F/gas mark 4).

2 Place the wholemeal flour in a large bowl and sieve in the plain flour, cream of tartar, baking soda and salt. Stir in the sugar, chopped prunes and walnuts.

3 In a separate bowl, add the milk and egg to the melted margarine. Beat lightly with a fork to break up the egg.

4 Make a well in the centre of the dry ingredients and pour in the wet ingredients. Stir well to combine and transfer to the loaf tin. Place at the top of the preheated oven and bake for 50 minutes to 1 hour, until a skewer inserted into the centre comes out clean. Remove from the tin and leave to cool on a wire rack.

15

♥ = heart healthy   🍎 = counts towards 5-a-day   ✗ = lower fat

Rye bread

This bread is very easy to make as instant yeast means that it only needs to be left to prove (rise) once. This is delicious with banana or cheese and is especially handy for breakfast as the dough can be prepared to the proving stage in the evening and left overnight in the fridge.

PREPARATION TIME: less than 30 minutes + proving time
COOKING TIME: 30–60 minutes
MAKES 2 loaves

100 ml (3½ fl oz) runny honey
4 tsp vegetable oil
250 g (9 oz) rye flour
350 g (12½ oz) strong wholemeal flour
1 tsp salt
3 dsp caraway seeds
1 sachet (7 g/¼ oz) instant yeast

1 Pour the honey into a jug and add around 150 ml (5 fl oz) boiling water. Allow the honey to dissolve, stirring occasionally. When dissolved, add another 150 ml (5 fl oz) cold water and add the oil. The liquid should be about hand hot.

2 Sieve the flours and salt into a roomy bowl, add the caraway seeds and sprinkle over the yeast. Mix thoroughly. Then make a well in the centre of the flour and pour in most of the honey liquid. Using a metal spoon or your hand, combine the flour and the liquid by stirring in a circular motion when rotating the bowl. Add the remaining liquid when most of the flour is incorporated and then continue to add warm water as needed to form a dough that is firm but not sticky. You will probably need 350–400 ml (12–14 fl oz) in total.

3 Flour the work surface with wholemeal flour and turn out the dough. Knead for about 10 minutes, until the dough becomes smooth and elastic. Return to a greased bowl, cover with a clean tea towel and set aside in a warm, draught-free place until the dough has doubled in volume.

4 Preheat the oven to 180° C (350° F/gas mark 4). Tip the dough out onto the floured surface and lightly punch the air out of the dough. Split into two equal pieces, giving each ball of dough a quick knead and then place each piece in a 2-lb loaf tin. Bake for 40–50 minutes, until the loaves sound hollow when tapped on the bottom. Remove from the tins and leave to cool on a wire rack.

V = suitable for vegetarians   X = gluten free   X = dairy free   = source of fibre

Orange and poppyseed muffins

These muffins are very substantial! One will keep you going until lunchtime, especially if you have a perfectly balanced breakfast by having a glass of fruit juice and a small yoghurt too.

PREPARATION TIME: less than 20 minutes

COOKING TIME: less than 30 minutes

MAKES 12 muffins

1 orange
75 ml (2½ fl oz) vegetable oil
150 ml (5 fl oz) semi-skimmed milk
2 eggs
300 g (10½ oz) wholemeal flour
125 g (4½ oz) plain flour
4 level tsp baking powder
75 g (2½ oz) caster sugar
2 Tbsp poppy seeds

1 Line a 12-hole muffin tin with muffin cases (a silicone muffin tray will not need to be lined) and preheat the oven to 180° C (350° F/gas mark 4).

2 In a bowl, grate the zest of the orange and squeeze out the juice – there should be about 100 ml (3½ fl oz) of juice. Add in the oil, milk and eggs, and beat lightly with a fork to break up the eggs.

3 Place the wholemeal flour in a large bowl and sieve in the plain flour and baking powder. Stir in the sugar and poppy seeds. Make a well in the centre of the dry ingredients and pour in the wet ingredients. Stir to just combine and spoon into the prepared muffin tin.

4 Place at the top of the preheated oven and bake for 20 minutes, until the muffins are springy to the touch and a skewer inserted into the centre comes out clean. Remove from the tin and leave on a wire rack to cool.

♥ = heart healthy   🍎 = counts towards 5-a-day   ✗ = lower fat

Strawberry and brazil nut muffins

Muffins are perfect when you're in a rush as they can be made at the weekend and kept in the freezer – simply defrost for 1 minute or so in the microwave. Add a carton of fruit juice for a satisfying brekkie.

PREPARATION TIME: less than 20 minutes
COOKING TIME: less than 30 minutes
MAKES 12 muffins

1 pear
250 g (9 oz) wholegrain flour
75 g (2½ oz) plain flour
4 level tsp baking powder
Pinch salt
50 g (2 oz) brazil nuts, chopped
230 g (8 oz) strawberries, sliced
2 dsp runny honey
2 dsp vegetable oil
200 ml (7 fl oz) semi-skimmed milk
120 ml (4 fl oz) low-fat natural yoghurt
2 eggs

1 Line a 12-hole muffin tin with muffin cases (a silicone muffin tray will not need to be lined) and preheat the oven to 180° C (350° F/gas mark 4).

2 Peel the pear and cut into small pieces. Cook for 1 minute on high in the microwave or in a small saucepan for 3–4 minutes until slightly softened. Set aside to cool slightly.

3 Place the wholemeal flour in a large bowl and sieve in the plain flour and baking powder. Stir in the salt, chopped brazil nuts and sliced strawberries.

4 Add the honey, oil, milk, yoghurt and eggs to the pear. Beat lightly with a fork to break up the eggs.

5 Make a well in the centre of the dry ingredients and pour in the wet ingredients. Stir to just combine and spoon into the prepared muffin tin. Place at the top of the preheated oven and bake for 20 minutes, until the muffins are springy to the touch and a skewer inserted into the centre comes out clean. Remove from the tin and leave on a wire rack to cool.

18

V = suitable for vegetarians X = gluten free X = dairy free = source of fibre

Cranberry and macadamia yeast bread

This is another bread that can be made in the bread machine instead of by hand. Just follow manufacturer's guidelines as to the order in which to add ingredients. Use any combination of fruit and nuts that you have in the larder!

PREPARATION TIME: less than 30 minutes + proving time

COOKING TIME: 30–60 minutes

MAKES 1 loaf

260 ml (9½ fl oz) lukewarm water
½ tsp caster sugar
2 tsp dried yeast
400 g (14 oz) wholemeal flour
1 scant tsp salt
100 g (3½ oz) dried cranberries, chopped
75 g (2½ oz) macadamia nuts, chopped
1 Tbsp melted butter

19

1 Pour the water into a jug (the water needs to be around body temperature), add the sugar and sprinkle over the dried yeast. Set aside for around 10 minutes to sponge, that is, until a beery head forms.

2 Place the flour and salt into a large bowl and stir in the chopped cranberries and macadamia nuts. Make a well in the centre and pour in the sponged yeast along with the melted butter. Stir with a wooden spoon to combine – the dough should be moist and firm but not sticky. Place the dough on a floured work surface and knead gently for about 5 minutes, until the dough becomes smooth. Place in a large bowl and either set somewhere warm for around 2 hours, or place in the fridge overnight. The dough will double in volume.

3 After this time, preheat the oven to 220° C (425° F/gas mark 7) and line a 2-lb loaf tin with baking parchment. Give the dough another light knead, just for a couple of minutes, and place in the tin. Bake in the preheated oven for 10 minutes, then lower the heat to 190° C (375° F/gas mark 5) and bake for a further 30–40 minutes, until the bread sounds hollow when tapped on the bottom. Remove from the tin and leave to cool on a wire rack.

♥ = heart healthy   🍎 = counts towards 5-a-day   ✕ = lower fat

Porridge with fruit compote

Porridge is a low-medium GI breakfast and is a great source of insoluble fibre. This is fibre that dissolves in the body to form a kind of gel, and this gel absorbs unhealthy LDL cholesterol. So eating porridge every morning can help improve your cholesterol balance. Add a fruit compote for a perfectly balanced breakfast.

PREPARATION TIME: less than 10 minutes
COOKING TIME: less than 10 minutes
SERVES 2

⅔ teacup of porridge oats
⅓ teacup of water
⅔ teacup of semi-skimmed milk

Combine the oats, water and milk in a small saucepan and bring to the boil. Simmer for around 5 minutes until thickened. Alternatively place all the ingredients in a microwave-safe jug and cook on high for 3 minutes. Top with a little milk and honey or with one of the fruit compotes featured here.

Apple and pear compote 𝒱 ✕ 🌾 🍎 ✕

This is a lovely warm compote for autumn and winter. Make double or even triple amounts and keep it in the fridge so it's ready to top porridge for weekday breakfasts.

Peel 1 apple and 1 pear and cut into 2-cm (¾-in) pieces. Place the apple pieces into a small saucepan with 10 g (⅓ oz) butter and ½ tablespoon of lemon juice and cook gently for 4 minutes. Add the pear pieces, ½ teaspoon of runny honey and a good pinch of allspice and continue to cook gently for 8–10 minutes.

𝒱 = suitable for vegetarians   ✕ = gluten free   ✕ = dairy free   🌾 = source of fibre

Summer berry compote

Use a mix of berries to get a mix of nutrients! And instead of abandoning fruit come winter, use fruit tinned in juice or quick frozen fruit instead. Fresh is best but preserved is a very close second! Try this compote as a topping for your morning porridge.

1 Rinse 230 g (8 oz) mixed berries (including strawberries, raspberries and blackberries) and place them in a small saucepan. Sprinkle over 1 teaspoon of vanilla sugar and add just a splash of water. Bring to the boil and simmer for 5 minutes, until the fruit is broken down. Set aside to cool slightly.

2 In a small bowl or cup, add a splash of cold water to 1 teaspoon of arrowroot and stir well to mix. Stir into the fruit, return to the heat and bring back to the boil, stirring gently all the time. For a dessert compote, try adding a dash of fruit liqueur such as cassis to the fruit instead of water.

21

Fig and prune compote

Even if you don't have time to go shopping for fresh fruit, you needn't miss out on your 5-a-day! Simply simmer dried fruit in orange juice and use to top porridge or stir into yoghurt.

Cut 4 dried figs and 6 stoned prunes into bite-sized pieces and place in a small saucepan with 4 tablespoons of orange juice and ½ cinnamon stick. Bring to the boil and simmer gently for 15 minutes.

 = heart healthy　　 = counts towards 5-a-day　　 = lower fat

Granola

Granola is a baked version of muesli, so you get the same healthy mix of oats, nuts and fruit but with a honey-sweetened crunch!

PREPARATION TIME: less than 10 minutes
COOKING TIME: 30–60 minutes
SERVES 8

150 g (5½ oz) jumbo rolled oats
30 g (1 oz) almonds, chopped
30 g (1 oz) pecan nuts, chopped
1 Tbsp runny honey
1 Tbsp vegetable oil
Pinch of salt
50 g (2 oz) sultanas
50 g (2 oz) dried cranberries

22

Preheat the oven to 180° C (350° F/gas mark 4). Place the oats, nuts, honey and oil in a bowl and mix to combine, leaving some chunkier pieces. Transfer to a non-stick baking tray, shake so the mix is in a single layer and place in the oven for 5 minutes. Decrease the heat to 140° C (275° F/gas mark 1) and continue to cook for 30 minutes. Leave to cool on the baking tray before stirring in the sultanas and cranberries. Store in an air-tight tin for up to two weeks.

Flapjacks

Flapjacks are ideal for a breakfast on the run and also make great snack bars. So forget commercially-made cereal bars and experiment with flapjacks instead! Wrap them in greaseproof paper and pop them into the kids' lunchboxes too.

PREPARATION TIME: less than 10 minutes
COOKING TIME: less than 30 minutes
MAKES 12 squares

1 cooking apple
75 g (2½ oz) polyunsaturated margarine
100 g (3½ oz) porridge oats
50 g (2 oz) millet
2 dsp runny honey
Pinch of salt
30 g (1 oz) sunflower seeds
20 g (¾ oz) flaxseeds
50 g (2 oz) sultanas
2 dried figs, chopped

23

1 Preheat the oven to 200° C (400° F/gas mark 6). Peel and core the apple and cut it into thin slices. Place in a small pan with 1 tablespoon of water and simmer for 5–10 minutes. Alternatively, place in a microwave-safe bowl and cook on high for around 3 minutes.

2 In a separate pan, melt the margarine, remove from the heat, and stir in all the other ingredients, including the stewed apple. Transfer to a 20-cm (8-in) square baking tin, flatten down firmly with the back of a spoon and cook for 10 minutes. Reduce the heat to 180° C (350° F/gas mark 4) and cook for a further 20 minutes. Allow to cool completely in the tin before cutting into squares.

= heart healthy   = counts towards 5-a-day   X = lower fat

starters

Warm rocket salad with red onions and pancetta

Salads don't need to be confined to summer! This warm salad is ideal to brighten up a winter day – just remember to take the salad leaves out of the fridge in advance. Rocket has a lovely peppery flavour so you needn't add too much pepper to the salad dressing.

PREPARATION TIME: less than 10 minutes
COOKING TIME: less than 30 minutes
SERVES 4

For the dressing:
2 Tbsp extra virgin olive oil
1 Tbsp balsamic vinegar
Freshly ground black pepper

For the salad:
100 g (3½ oz) rocket
4 red onions, peeled
2 tsp light olive oil
100 g (3½ oz) thinly sliced pancetta
Juice of ½ lemon

1 To prepare the salad dressing, combine all the dressing ingredients in a jam jar, seal and shake well. Taste and season with a little black pepper.

2 Wash the rocket and place it in a large bowl. Preheat a cast iron griddle pan. Cut the red onions into quarters through the root so each quarter stays intact. Brush with a little light olive oil and place, cut-side down, on the griddle pan. Cook for 4 minutes without moving, then turn onto the other cut surface. Cook for a further 4 minutes, until lightly caramelized. Set to one side of the pan and then add the strips of pancetta to the pan. Cook over a high heat, turning once, until crisp, for about 4 minutes.

3 Add the caramelized onions and pancetta to the salad bowl and toss in the dressing. Arrange on four plates and drizzle with a little lemon juice.

$\mathcal{V}$ = suitable for vegetarians   ✗ = gluten free   ✗ = dairy free   = source of fibre

Beetroot and feta salad

Too many of us consign beetroot to the pickle jar when, in fact,
it makes for delicious salads. It is rich in folate, potassium and
manganese and the tops can also be added to the salad to provide
extra calcium, beta-carotene and iron. Be sure to add the feta
cheese to this salad at the last minute – otherwise you'll end up
with pink cheese!

PREPARATION TIME: less than 10 minutes
COOKING TIME: less than 10 minutes
SERVES 4

2 Tbs pine nuts

For the dressing:
2 Tbsp extra virgin olive oil
1 Tbsp balsamic vinegar
½ Tbsp white wine vinegar
1 tsp grain mustard, preferably Dijon
Salt and freshly ground black pepper

For the salad:
1 bag of mixed rocket, watercress
    and spinach salad
4 vacuum-packed cooked beetroot
100 g (3½ oz) feta cheese

1 Heat a small frying pan and add the pine nuts. Dry-fry for 5–6 minutes, stirring
occasionally until the pine nuts are golden and aromatic. Keep watching these
as they burn easily. Set aside on a plate to cool.

2 To prepare the salad dressing, combine all the dressing ingredients in a jam
jar, seal and shake well. Taste and season with salt and a little black pepper.
Remember the rocket leaves in the salad will be peppery.

3 To make the salad, wash the salad leaves and arrange on four plates.
Cut the beetroot in half, and then each half into three and arrange over the
leaves. Crumble over the feta cheese and sprinkle with the toasted pine nuts.
Drizzle a couple of teaspoons of dressing over each plate before serving.

♥ = heart healthy   = counts towards 5-a-day   = lower fat

Mixed beans with olives, red onion and parsley

This recipe uses barlotti, cannellini and haricot beans, but it's fine to use whatever you have in the cupboard or to use a tin of mixed beans. Just be sure to drain this well and rinse under cold water to remove excess sugar and salt.

28

PREPARATION TIME: less than 10 minutes
COOKING TIME: none
SERVES 4

For the dressing:
2 Tbsp extra virgin olive oil
1½ Tbsp red wine vinegar
1 clove of garlic, peeled and crushed with a pinch of salt
Pinch of brown sugar
Freshly ground black pepper

For the salad:
1 small red onion, peeled and finely sliced
150 g (5½ oz) each of cooked barlotti, cannellini and haricot beans
6 sun-dried tomatoes in oil
20 olives, a mix of varieties including kalamata, queens and dry cured
Small bunch of flat leaf parsley

Toasted multi-grain baguette, to serve

1 To make the dressing, combine all the dressing ingredients in a jam jar, seal and shake well. Season with a little black pepper. The olives and sun-dried tomatoes will be salty so you shouldn't need to add any salt to the dressing.

2 To make the salad, place the red onion in a bowl and pour over enough boiling water to cover. Set aside for a couple of minutes, then drain through a sieve. This will take the raw edge off the onion.

3 Combine all the salad ingredients in a large bowl and toss with the prepared dressing. Serve at room temperature with toasted baguette slices: cut a multi-grain baguette into slices on the diagonal. Toast under the grill and then rub the surface with the cut side of a clove of garlic.

V = suitable for vegetarians   X = gluten free   X = dairy free   = source of fibre

Chicken liver pâté

This is the ideal starter for a dinner party as it can be made well in advance and refrigerated until needed. Just be sure to take it out of the fridge an hour or so before you want to serve it. This pâté is much lighter than traditional recipes as cottage cheese is used instead of cream and it doesn't have the usual butter topping.

PREPARATION TIME: less than 10 minutes
COOKING TIME: less than 30 minutes
SERVES 4

1 tsp olive oil
1 shallot, peeled and finely chopped
1 clove of garlic, peeled and crushed
250 g (9 oz) chicken livers, trimmed
Good pinch of dried sage
¼ tsp allspice or 1 allspice berry, crushed
1 Tbsp Marsala or Madeira
2 Tbsp cottage cheese
Toasted multi-grain baguette, to serve

29

1 Heat the oil in a non-stick frying pan and add the shallot and garlic. Cook for 5–6 minutes to soften without colouring. Add the chicken livers, sage, allspice and Marsala or Madeira and cook for a further 10 minutes. Set aside to cool.

2 When almost cool, transfer to a food processor and add the cottage cheese. Process until the pâté is smooth. Spoon into individual ramekins or another serving dish and refrigerate. Remove from the fridge 30 minutes to 1 hour before serving.

3 Serve with toasted baguette slices: cut a multi-grain baguette into slices on the diagonal. Toast under the grill and then rub the surface with the cut side of a clove of garlic.

= heart healthy　= counts towards 5-a-day　= lower fat

Mushroom and walnut pâté

Dried mushrooms are available in most supermarkets – either bags of mixed mushrooms or porcini. These will keep for a few months and so are a handy store-cupboard staple – they lend a lovely earthy flavour to pasta sauces, risotto and, of course, pâté.

PREPARATION TIME: less than 10 minutes + soaking time
COOKING TIME: less than 30 minutes
SERVES 4–6

50 g (2 oz) walnuts
25 g (1 oz) dried mushrooms
2 tsp olive oil
10 g (⅓ oz) butter
1 small onion, peeled and finely chopped
1 clove of garlic, peeled and crushed
350 g (12½ oz) button mushrooms, sliced
Pinch of dried thyme
2 Tbsp extra light cream cheese
Toasted multi-grain baguette, to serve

1 Heat a small frying pan and add the walnuts. Dry-fry for 6–8 minutes, stirring occasionally until they are toasted and aromatic. Keep watching these as they burn easily. Set aside on a plate to cool.

2 Place the dried mushrooms in a bowl and pour over enough boiling water to cover. Set aside to soak for 20 minutes.

3 After this time, drain off the soaking water and pour the liquid into a wide frying pan. Bring to the boil until the volume is reduced to 1–2 tablespoons. Pour this liquid into a cup and set aside.

4 Using the same frying pan, heat the olive oil and butter together. Add the onion and garlic and cook for 5–6 minutes to soften without colouring. Add the fresh mushrooms and thyme and cook for 8–10 minutes. Chop the re-hydrated mushrooms and add to the pan, along with the reserved soaking liquid. Cook for a further 10 minutes to allow excess liquid to reduce. Set aside to cool slightly.

𝒱 = suitable for vegetarians   ✗ = gluten free   ✗ = dairy free   = source of fibre

5 When almost cool, transfer to a food processor and add the toasted walnuts along with the cream cheese. Process until the pâté is almost smooth. Spoon into individual ramekins or another serving dish and refrigerate. Remove from the fridge 1 hour before serving.

6 Serve with toasted baguette slices: cut a multi-grain baguette into slices on the diagonal. Toast under the grill and then rub the surface with the cut side of a clove of garlic.

Spicy bean pâté

This makes a good starter for a Mexican-style meal and is a good vegetarian alternative to other pâtés. It's very versatile – serve with Spiced pitta chips (p 69), as a filling for pitta bread or as a spread for tortillas. It's also a quick snack spread on wholegrain toast!

PREPARATION TIME: less than 10 minutes
COOKING TIME: less than 10 minutes
SERVES 4–8

1 tsp olive oil
1 onion, peeled and chopped
2 cloves of garlic, peeled and crushed
1 tsp chilli powder, hot or mild to your preference
⅓ tsp smoked paprika
⅓ tsp dried oregano
150 g (5⅓ oz) each of cooked pinto, haricot and red kidney beans
    (or use a 400-g/14-oz tin of mixed beans, drained and rinsed)
Juice of 1 lime
Small bunch of fresh coriander

1 Heat the oil in a non-stick frying pan and add the onion and crushed garlic. Cook for 5–6 minutes to soften without colouring. Add the chilli powder, paprika and oregano and stir into the onions. Add the beans and the juice of the lime and cook for just 2–3 minutes. Set aside to cool slightly.

2 When almost cool, transfer to a food processor, add the fresh coriander and process until the ingredients are well combined but not too smooth.

♥ = heart healthy   🍎 = counts towards 5-a-day   ✗ = lower fat

Salmon dip

Like other oily fish, salmon is a rich source of essential fatty acids – the fatty acids found in mono- and polyunsaturated fats. We should aim to eat at least one portion of oily fish every week, as well as a portion of white fish, and most people would benefit from eating 3 or 4 portions per week. The exception is pregnant and breastfeeding women who shouldn't eat more than one portion of oily fish each week.

PREPARATION TIME: less than 30 minutes
COOKING TIME: none
SERVES 8–10 as a dip

400 g (14 oz) tinned pink salmon, skin and bones removed
200 ml (7 fl oz) reduced fat crème fraîche
1 tsp horseradish
1 Tbsp capers
1 Tbsp fresh dill
Juice of ½ lemon
Sprig of fresh dill
Oatcakes and vegetable sticks, to serve

Combine all the ingredients in the bowl of a food processor and process until just combined. Transfer to a serving bowl and top with a sprig of fresh dill. Serve as a dip with oatcakes and vegetable sticks.

$\mathcal{V}$ = suitable for vegetarians   ✗ = gluten free   ✗ = dairy free   = source of fibre

Red pesto cream cheese dip

Sun-dried tomatoes are available both in jars of olive oil and dehydrated, in bags. For this recipe, use the dehydrated version as the cream cheese and pesto both provide fat – using tomatoes in oil would add a lot more fat and calories to the dish.

PREPARATION TIME: less than 10 minutes + soaking time

COOKING TIME: none

SERVES 8–10 as a dip

4 sun-dried tomatoes (dehydrated)
200 g (7 oz) extra light cream cheese
1 Tbsp red pesto
Small bunch of fresh basil

1 Place the sun-dried tomatoes into a small bowl and pour over enough boiling water to just cover. Set aside to soak for 15–20 minutes. After this time, drain the tomatoes and cut into small pieces.

2 Place the cream cheese into a bowl and stir in the chopped tomatoes, pesto and torn basil. Mix well before serving as a dip for vegetable sticks, as a topping for wholegrain crackers or as a stuffing for mild piquant peppers.

33

♥ = heart healthy　🍎 = counts towards 5-a-day　X = lower fat

Beetroot dip

If you like hummus, you'll love this dip! Serve it with toasted wholegrain pitta bread, on oatcakes or with vegetable sticks.

PREPARATION TIME: less than 10 minutes

COOKING TIME: none

SERVES 2

2 beetroot, vacuum-packed is fine
1 clove of garlic, peeled
1 Tbsp natural yoghurt
1 dsp tahini
Juice of ¼ lemon
Sesame seeds

34

Combine all the ingredients, except the sesame seeds, in a food processor and blitz until smooth. Spoon into a serving dish and top with a sprinkling of sesame seeds.

Green pesto cream cheese dip

This pesto-flavoured cream cheese makes a great dip for vegetable sticks, can be used as a topping for wholegrain crackers or as a stuffing for mild piquant peppers or baby plum tomatoes.

𝒱
Ӿ

PREPARATION TIME: less than 10 minutes

COOKING TIME: none

SERVES 8–10 as a dip

200 g (7 oz) extra light cream cheese
1 Tbsp green pesto
6 black or green olives (or a mix of both), finely chopped
Small bunch of fresh basil
Freshly ground black pepper

Place the cream cheese into a bowl and stir in the pesto, olives and torn basil. Season with freshly ground black pepper and mix well before serving.

𝒱 = suitable for vegetarians   Ӿ = gluten free   Ӿ = dairy free   = source of fibre

Roast pepper and walnut dip

A couple of more unusual ingredients are used here – pomegranate molasses and sumac. These can both be found in specialist delis but it would be fine to replace pomegranate molasses with half the amount of black treacle and instead of using sumac, try adding a half teaspoon each of cinnamon and cumin. This can be served in a similar way to hummus, on pitta bread or with vegetable sticks.

PREPARATION TIME: less than 10 minutes

COOKING TIME: 30–60 minutes

SERVES 4

2 red peppers
6 cloves of garlic, unpeeled
Extra virgin olive oil
75 g (2½ oz) walnuts
2 tsp pomegranate molasses
1 tsp sumac

35

1 Preheat the oven to 200° C (400° F/gas mark 6). Cut the peppers into thirds, removing the seeds and pith and place on a baking tray. Tuck the unpeeled garlic cloves in and around the peppers and drizzle with extra virgin olive oil. Roast for 25–30 minutes, until the peppers are soft and beginning to colour at the edges.

2 Place the walnuts on a separate baking tray and place these in the oven to toast during the last 8 minutes or so of the roasting time. Combine the roast peppers, peeled roast garlic, toasted walnuts, pomegranate molasses and sumac in a food processor and blitz until the dip is not quite smooth.

soups

Sweet potato and lentil soup

Sweet potatoes lend a delicious sweetness to this soup – but they also provide huge amounts of nutrients. One small sweet potato provides three times our daily requirements of vitamin A, in the form of beta-carotene, and provides significant amounts of vitamin C, manganese, copper, fibre, vitamin B6, potassium and iron. All this and they have a low to medium GI value.

PREPARATION TIME: less than 10 minutes
COOKING TIME: less than 30 minutes
SERVES 4

1 tsp olive oil
1 tsp mustard seeds (a mix of yellow and black)
1 onion, peeled and finely chopped
2 cloves of garlic, peeled and crushed
400 g (14 oz) sweet potato, peeled
1 red chilli, finely chopped
½ tsp fenugreek
½ tsp ground ginger
1 tsp turmeric
150 g (5½ oz) red lentils
400 g (14 oz) chopped tinned tomatoes
400 ml (14 fl oz) vegetable stock
Salt and white pepper
Small bunch of fresh coriander, chopped
4 Tbsp of natural yoghurt

1 Heat the oil in a large saucepan and add the mustard seeds. When the seeds pop, add the onion and garlic and cook for 5–6 minutes to soften without colouring.

2 Cut the sweet potato into 2-cm (¾-in) pieces and add to the pan, along with the chilli and the remaining spices and continue to cook until the spices become aromatic. Stir in the lentils, tomatoes and pour in the stock. Season with a little salt and white pepper and bring to the boil, then simmer for 20 minutes.

3 Sprinkle with chopped fresh coriander and a spoonful of natural yoghurt before serving.

38

𝒱 = suitable for vegetarians   X = gluten free   X = dairy free   = source of fibre

Rosebud's broth

This is a traditional broth made using soup mix – a mixture of barley, red lentils and split peas. If you can't find soup mix, make your own by combining two parts barley to one part each of split peas and red lentils. This soup makes a very satisfying lunch with a slice of wheaten bread with mature cheddar.

PREPARATION TIME: 10–20 minutes
COOKING TIME: 30–60 minutes
SERVES 4

1 tsp vegetable oil
10 g (⅓ oz) butter
1 small leek, sliced
2 stalks of celery, including leaves, sliced
1 medium carrot, diced
100 g (3½ oz) soup mix
600 ml (1 pint) vegetable stock
30 g (1 oz) curly parsley
Salt and freshly ground black pepper

39

1 Heat the oil and butter together in a large pan and add the leeks and celery, setting the celery leaves aside. Cover and sweat over a low heat for 8–10 minutes. Add the carrot and soup mix and stir well. Pour in the stock and the finely chopped parsley stalks, setting the leaves aside. Season with salt and a little pepper and simmer for 40 minutes.

2 After this time, add the roughly chopped parsley and celery leaves and simmer for a further 5 minutes.

♥ = heart healthy   = counts towards 5-a-day   ✕ = lower fat

Split green pea soup with herb yoghurt

This is a thick and warming soup, perfect for a dull winter's day – the vibrant herb yoghurt will bring a little colour to the day! Soups are often garnished or made with cream but this adds unnecessary fat and calories. Yoghurt is the ideal low fat way to lighten up the soup.

PREPARATION TIME: less than 10 minutes

COOKING TIME: 30–60 minutes

SERVES 4

For the soup:
2 tsp olive oil
1 onion, peeled and roughly chopped
2 cloves of garlic, peeled and crushed
300 g (10½ oz) split green peas
600 ml (1 pint) vegetable stock

For the herb yoghurt:
2 Tbsp finely chopped parsley
2 Tbsp finely chopped mint
2 Tbsp finely chopped coriander
1 clove of garlic, peeled and crushed
1 level tsp paprika
4 Tbsp natural yoghurt

1 To make the soup, heat the oil in a large saucepan and add the onion and garlic. Cook for 4 minutes to soften slightly. Add the split green peas and stir to coat in oil. Pour in the stock, bring to the boil, then simmer for 45 minutes.

2 In the meantime, prepare the herb yoghurt. In a bowl, stir the herbs, garlic and the paprika into the yoghurt and refrigerate until needed.

3 Once the peas are tender, blitz with a hand-held immersion blender or in the food processor. Serve the soup topped with a spoonful of herb yoghurt.

40

= suitable for vegetarians   = gluten free   = dairy free   = source of fibre

Roast vegetable soup

This soup is a fantastic way towards your 5-a-day and roasting the vegetables before combining them in a soup intensifies their flavour and sweetness. This means even confirmed veggie haters will enjoy it! This soup also characterizes the heart-healthy Mediterranean diet since it's jam-packed with vegetables and olive oil.

PREPARATION TIME: less than 10 minutes
COOKING TIME: 1 hour or more
SERVES 5–6

1 onion, peeled
1 red onion, peeled
1 green pepper
½ red pepper
½ yellow pepper
½ aubergine
4 ripe plum tomatoes
4 cloves of garlic, peeled
Few sprigs of thyme
1-2 Tbsp extra virgin olive oil
Salt and freshly ground black pepper
600 ml (1 pint) vegetable stock

41

1 Preheat the oven to 200° C (400° F/gas mark 6). Chop the vegetables into approximately 3-cm (1½-in) pieces, place them on a baking tray and tuck the garlic cloves (peeled but not crushed) and the thyme in among the vegetables. Drizzle with the extra virgin olive oil. Place high in the preheated oven and roast for 20–30 minutes, until the vegetables are just beginning to char at the edges.

2 Once cooked, transfer all the vegetables, along with any juices in the tray into a large saucepan. Season with a little salt and plenty of freshly ground black pepper. Add the vegetable stock and bring to the boil. Simmer for 20 minutes, remove the thyme stalks, then blend, either using the blender attachment of the food processor or a hand-held immersion blender.

= heart healthy   = counts towards 5-a-day   = lower fat

Sweet potato and coconut soup

Most nuts are good sources of healthy unsaturated fats – coconut is the exception to the rule. Weight for weight, coconut has almost six times as much saturated fat as minced beef and only a fraction – one seventh – of the protein of almonds. This is why it's so great to see reduced fat coconut milk on the supermarket shelves as this will have at least ⅓ less fat than regular coconut milk.

PREPARATION TIME: less than 10 minutes
COOKING TIME: less than 30 minutes
SERVES 4

2 medium-large or 3 small sweet potatoes (around 450 g/1 lb in total), peeled
1 small shallot, peeled and roughly chopped
2 red chillis, or to taste, sliced
2-cm (¾-in) piece of fresh ginger, peeled and cut into coins
2 stalks of lemongrass
400 ml (14 fl oz) reduced fat coconut milk
200 ml (7 fl oz) light vegetable stock
Juice of 1 lime
Bunch of coriander, chopped

1 Cut the sweet potatoes into 3–4-cm (1½-in) pieces. Place in a large saucepan along with the shallot, chillis and ginger. Remove the outer woody stems from the lemongrass and bruise the inner stems with the handle of your knife, then add these to the pan. Pour in the coconut milk and stock – it's easiest just to half-fill the coconut milk tin with boiling water and stir in 1 heaped teaspoon of good vegetable stock powder. Squeeze in the juice of half the lime.

2 Bring to the boil, then simmer for 15–20 minutes, until the sweet potato chunks are tender. Remove the lemongrass and blend, either using the blender attachment of the food processor or a hand-held immersion blender. As you liquidize, you'll see the white coconut milk change to a vibrant orange!

3 Have a taste test and add a little more lime juice to taste and sprinkle with freshly chopped coriander when serving.

𝒱 = suitable for vegetarians   ✗ = gluten free   ✗ = dairy free   = source of fibre

Minestrone

Making minestrone is a great way to use up leftovers. In fact, minestrone was originally made as a way to avoid wasting food and so recipes for minestrone vary considerably. One thing they all have in common is the large amount of vegetables used. Beans are almost always added, as is pasta or rice. This recipe also uses the Italian cured bacon, pancetta. If you can't find pancetta, smoked streaky bacon will give a nice depth of flavour to the soup. Vary this recipe depending on what you have in the fridge and what's in season.

PREPARATION TIME: less than 20 minutes
COOKING TIME: 1 hour or more
SERVES 6

2 tsp olive oil
1 medium-large onion, peeled and finely chopped
2 small or 1 medium-large carrot, diced
2 stalks of celery, diced
50 g (2 oz) pancetta, or 4 rashers of smoked streaky bacon
800 g (1 lb 12 oz) tinned chopped tomatoes
400 ml (14 fl oz) vegetable stock
400 g (14 oz) tinned mixed beans, drained and rinsed
Freshly ground black pepper
1 tsp dried mixed herbs, or herbes de Provence
100 g (3½ oz) pasta shapes such as fusilli

43

1 Heat the olive oil in a large pan and add the vegetables. Cook on a high heat for 1–2 minutes, then reduce the heat, cover and allow the vegetables to sweat for 8–10 minutes, stirring occasionally.

2 Cut the pancetta into 1-cm (½-in) cubes or the bacon into 2-cm (¾-in) pieces and add to the vegetables in the pan. Increase the heat a little to cook off the pancetta or bacon.

3 Pour in the tomatoes, stock and beans. Season with plenty of freshly ground black pepper and mixed herbs. Bring to the boil and simmer gently for 40 minutes. After this time, add the pasta and continue to cook for a further 15–20 minutes or until the pasta is al dente.

♥ = heart healthy   🍎 = counts towards 5-a-day   ✗ = lower fat

Sausage and bean soup

Kielbasa is a Polish sausage, and can now be found in many supermarkets with other specialty meats. If you can't find kielbasa, it's fine to use any other well-flavoured sausage or salami you enjoy.

PREPARATION TIME: less than 10 minutes
COOKING TIME: 30–60 minutes
SERVES 6

1 tsp olive oil
1 medium-sized onion, peeled and finely chopped
2 fat cloves of garlic, peeled and crushed
150 g (5½ oz) kielbasa sausage
1 heaped tsp smoked paprika
400 g (14 oz) tinned chopped tomatoes
600 ml (1 pint) vegetable stock
400 g (14 oz) tinned kidney beans, drained and rinsed
Freshly ground black pepper
1 tsp dried thyme
Juice of ½ lemon
Reduced fat crème fraîche

44

1 Heat the olive oil in a large pan and add the onion. Cook over a high heat for 1–2 minutes, then add the garlic. Reduce the heat, cover and allow to sweat for 8–10 minutes, stirring occasionally.

2 Cut the kielbasa into coins and add to the pan, along with the smoked paprika. Increase the heat a little and cook for 3–4 minutes. Pour in the tomatoes, stock and beans. Season with plenty of freshly ground black pepper and add the thyme. Bring to the boil, then simmer gently for 40 minutes.

3 Ladle half the soup into a bowl and blend, either using the blender attachment of the food processor or a hand-held immersion blender. Return this to the rest of the soup and stir in – liquidizing half the soup will give a smoother texture while still retaining some character. Squeeze in the juice of half a lemon and top each bowl of soup with a heaped teaspoon of crème fraîche.

$\mathcal{V}$ = suitable for vegetarians   ✗ = gluten free   ✗ = dairy free   = source of fibre

Winter lentil soup with kale

Kale is a very under-valued vegetable – not only does it provide a warm, earthy flavour, but it is also one of the most nutrient-dense foods around. One serving provides almost twice our daily requirement for vitamin A, almost our full requirement of vitamin C, as well as a host of vitamins, minerals and sulphurophane, a compound that has powerful cancer-fighting properties. Green lentils will become soft and lose their shape on cooking more so than brown lentils, which will retain their shape and texture. The choice is yours!

PREPARATION TIME: less than 10 minutes
COOKING TIME: 1 hour or more
SERVES 4

3 leaves of curly kale
1 tsp olive oil
1 medium onion, peeled and finely chopped
1 medium carrot, diced
1 stalk of celery, diced
200 g (7 oz) green or brown lentils
1 tsp dried oregano
400 g (14 oz) tinned chopped tomatoes
400 ml (14 fl oz) vegetable stock
Dash of balsamic vinegar

45

1 Cut the tough stems from the kale and cut these into small cubes. Heat the olive oil in a large pan and add the onion, carrot, celery and kale stems. Cook over a high heat for 1–2 minutes, then reduce the heat, cover and allow the vegetables to sweat for 8–10 minutes, stirring occasionally.

2 Stir in the lentils and oregano and cook for a couple of minutes. Pour in the tomatoes and stock, bring to the boil, then simmer for 30–40 minutes. After this time, add the sliced kale leaves, bring back to the boil and simmer for a further 5 minutes. Drizzle a teaspoon or so of balsamic vinegar into each bowl of soup when serving.

♥ = heart healthy   = counts towards 5-a-day   ✗ = lower fat

Fresh mint and pea soup

This is a lighter and more summery alternative to the Split green pea soup with herb and yoghurt on p 40. This can be made with fresh peas when they are in season, but using frozen peas means that, more often than not, you'll have the ingredients on hand to whip up a big pot of homemade soup. Fantastic!

PREPARATION TIME: less than 10 minutes

COOKING TIME: less than 30 minutes

SERVES 4

1 tsp light olive oil
1 small onion, peeled and finely chopped
2 small new potatoes, diced
750 g (1 lb 10 oz) frozen peas
500 ml (18 fl oz) light chicken or vegetable stock
Small bunch of mint
100 ml (3½ fl oz) semi-skimmed milk

1 Heat the olive oil in a large pan and add the onion and potatoes. Cook over a high heat for 1–2 minutes, then reduce the heat, cover and allow to sweat for 8–10 minutes, stirring occasionally.

2 Stir in the frozen peas and stock, bring to the boil, then simmer for 8–10 minutes. Roughly tear the mint leaves and add to the soup.

3 Blend the soup, either using the blender attachment of the food processor or a hand-held immersion blender. Return to the pan and add the milk. Heat through before serving.

$\mathcal{V}$ = suitable for vegetarians   X = gluten free   X = dairy free   = source of fibre

Rocket and goat's cheese soup

Rocket is more often to be found in the salad bowl than the soup bowl! But this peppery leaf makes a tasty soup that's also a good source of vitamins A and C, folate and calcium. If you can't find rocket (also known as arugula), use watercress or even baby spinach leaves instead.

PREPARATION TIME: less than 10 minutes
COOKING TIME: 10–30 minutes
SERVES 4

1 tsp olive oil
10 g (⅓ oz) butter
1 small leek, sliced
1 medium-large courgette, sliced
2 cloves of garlic, peeled and crushed
3 new potatoes, diced
600 ml (1 pint) vegetable stock
100 g (3½ oz) rocket
75 g (2½ oz) firm goat's cheese

47

1 Heat the oil and butter together in a large pan and add the leek, courgette, garlic and potatoes. Cook over a high heat for 1–2 minutes, then reduce the heat, cover and allow to sweat for 8–10 minutes, stirring occasionally.

2 Pour in the stock, bring to the boil, then simmer for 10 minutes. Stir in the rocket, bring back to the boil and simmer for a further 5 minutes. Blend the soup, either using the blender attachment of the food processor or a hand-held immersion blender. Crumble in the goat's cheese when serving.

♥ = heart healthy   🍎 = counts towards 5-a-day   ✗ = lower fat

Celery, leek and chickpea soup

This is a lovely warming soup. When blended, the chickpeas give texture and body to the soup but if you prefer you can, of course, leave the soup chunky. Or you might prefer to blend half the soup and stir this back into the pot, along with the milk. If you prefer a non-vegetarian version, pieces of spiced sausages wouldn't go amiss.

PREPARATION TIME: less than 10 minutes
COOKING TIME: 30–60 minutes
SERVES 4

10 g (⅓ oz) butter
1 tsp olive oil
150 g (5½ oz) leeks, sliced
250 g (9 oz) celery, sliced
2 cloves of garlic, peeled and finely chopped
200 g (7 oz) cooked chickpeas
1 tsp dried thyme
1 allspice berry, crushed
500 ml (18 fl oz) vegetable stock
Salt and freshly ground black pepper
100 ml (3½ fl oz) milk
Parmesan, to serve

1 Melt the butter and oil together in a large saucepan, add the leeks and cook over a medium-high heat for 4 minutes. Add the celery and cook for a further 4 minutes. Add the garlic, reduce the heat, then cover and allow to sweat for 6 minutes. Add the cooked chickpeas, thyme, allspice and stock, season well with salt and black pepper, bring to the boil, then simmer for 20 minutes.

2 Liquidize the soup using a hand-held immersion blender or food processor, gradually adding the milk. Reheat gently. Before serving, place a soup-spoonful of grated parmesan into each bowl.

$\mathcal{V}$ = suitable for vegetarians   X = gluten free   X = dairy free   = source of fibre

Noodle soup with pork

This is a very soothing soup. It's quick to make (even quicker if you want a vegetarian version), delicious to eat and has a certain feel-good factor! The amounts for flavourings given here are just guidelines – keep tasting the soup and seasoning to your own preferences.

PREPARATION TIME: 10 minutes + marinating time

COOKING TIME: less than 30 minutes

SERVES 2

For the pork marinade:
1 Tbsp soy sauce
1 Tbsp rice vinegar
1 red chilli, sliced
2 boneless pork chops, fat trimmed

For the stock:
450 ml (16 fl oz) of well-flavoured
   vegetable stock
4-cm (1½-in) piece of ginger,
   peeled and cut into coins
2 star anise
2 blocks of egg noodles
8 small florets of broccoli
½ tsp sesame oil
1 tsp soy sauce
1–2 tsp sweet chilli sauce
1 tsp nam pla

49

1 Start by marinating the pork: pour the soy sauce, rice vinegar and chilli into a glass or ceramic dish and add the pork, making sure it is coated with the marinade. Refrigerate for 1 hour.

2 After this time, preheat the grill and grill the pork chops for around 15 minutes, turning occasionally.

3 Whilst the meat is cooking, make the stock. Bring the stock to the boil in a large pan, along with the ginger and star anise. Add the noodles and cook for 4–5 minutes, as directed on the packet. Add the florets of broccoli during the last 2 minutes of cooking time. Cut the pork into thick strips and add to the soup. Finally, season the soup with the sesame oil, soy sauce, sweet chilli sauce and nam pla, to your own taste.

♥ = heart healthy   = counts towards 5-a-day   X = lower fat

Chestnut and ham soup

This soup is quite time consuming, but it's worth it. It's a lovely rich soup that's perfect for special occasions, especially Christmas. Chestnuts are available tinned or in vacuum packs. Unlike other nuts, they are extremely low in fat and calories but they do provide vitamin C and B vitamins.

PREPARATION TIME: 30 minutes + steeping time if necessary
COOKING TIME: 3 hours (or overnight)
SERVES 6

For the stock:
1 ham hock, soaked overnight
   in cold water if salted
1 small onion, peeled
1 small carrot
1 stalk of celery
2 bay leaves
6 peppercorns

For the soup:
1 tsp vegetable oil
1 medium onion, peeled and finely
   chopped
1 medium carrot, diced
1 stalk of celery, diced
4 allspice berries, crushed
200 g (7 oz) vacuum-packed chestnuts,
   roughly chopped

Single cream and chopped chives,
   to serve

1 Start by preparing the stock. Place the ham hock in a large saucepan along with the remaining stock ingredients, cover with water and bring to the boil. Skim off any scum that rises to the surface and leave to simmer gently for 2–3 hours. Alternatively, place all the stock ingredients in a slow cooker and leave on the low setting overnight. This is the most hassle-free way in the world to make stock!

2 Pour the stock into a bowl, allow the fat to settle and skim off the excess fat. Strip the ham from the hock and set aside.

3 To make the soup, heat the oil in a large pan and add the vegetables. Cook on a high heat for 1–2 minutes, then reduce the heat, cover and allow the vegetables to sweat for 8–10 minutes, stirring occasionally.

50

$\mathcal{V}$ = suitable for vegetarians   ✗ = gluten free   ✗ = dairy free   = source of fibre

4 Stir in the allspice berries, chestnuts and about half the ham from the hock, depending on how much meat was on the hock. Cook for a couple of minutes and then pour in 750 ml (1¼ pints) of the ham stock. Bring to the boil, then simmer for 40 minutes. The rest of the ham can be frozen in the stock and used to make a lovely pea and ham soup another time.

5 Blend the soup, either using the blender attachment of the food processor or a hand-held immersion blender. Top with a teaspoon of lightly whipped cream and chives before serving.

 = heart healthy   = counts towards 5-a-day   X = lower fat

salads and brown bags

Hummus

Hummus is easily available in most supermarkets, but commercially-made hummus usually contains a lot of oil. This healthier version replaces some of that oil with yoghurt so the dip is still moist but has a fraction of the fat.

PREPARATION TIME: less than 10 minutes

COOKING TIME: none

SERVES 4

3 cloves of garlic, peeled
200 g (7 oz) cooked chickpeas
1 dsp low-fat natural yoghurt
1 dsp tahini
1 dsp extra virgin olive oil
2 dsp lemon juice
4 dsp water

Whiz the garlic in the food processor to chop it up. Add the remaining ingredients and blitz until the hummus is not quite smooth. Try some of the variations below for a little extra kick!

Lemon and coriander hummus

Add the zest of half a lemon and a small bunch of coriander (leaves and stalks) to the ingredients listed above. Process as before.

Roast pepper hummus

1 Preheat the oven to 200° C (400° F/gas mark 6). Cut a red pepper into quarters, place on a baking tray and drizzle with a little extra virgin olive oil. Place high in the oven and roast for 20–30 minutes, until just beginning to brown at the edges.

2 If preferred, place the hot pepper slices in a plastic bag, seal and allow the skins to soften. They can then be easily peeled off. Add the roast pepper, with or without skins, to the processor with the ingredients listed above.

𝒱 = suitable for vegetarians   ✗ = gluten free   ✗ = dairy free   = source of fibre

Warm kidney bean and roast onion salad

Roasting onions, especially red onions, really brings out their sweetness and makes them a delicious addition to a warm salad. This is perfect for a dull day at the beginning of autumn or a crisp spring day when a cold salad just won't quite hit the spot.

PREPARATION TIME: less than 10 minutes
COOKING TIME: less than 30 minutes
SERVES 4

3 red onions
1 Tbsp extra virgin olive oil
400 g (14 oz) tinned kidney beans, drained and rinsed
Bag of mixed salad leaves, including rocket and lollo rosso
½ Tbsp balsamic vinegar
2 Tbsp chopped flat leaf parsley
½ lemon, optional

55

1 Preheat the oven to 190° C (375° F/gas mark 5). Peel the onions and cut them into quarters. Place them on a baking tray and drizzle with half the olive oil. Roast for 20 minutes, then add the kidney beans to the tray and cook for a further 5 minutes. The onions should be just beginning to char at the edges.

2 In the meantime, tear the salad leaves into manageable pieces and place in a large bowl. Add in the roast onions, warm kidney beans, along with any juices in the tray, the balsamic vinegar and parsley. Toss well together and squeeze over a little lemon juice if desired.

♥ = heart healthy   🍎 = counts towards 5-a-day   ✕ = lower fat

Pesto cottage cheese

Cottage cheese is a great low fat protein source and a staple for many people at lunch time, but it can get a little boring. Enrich and enliven cottage cheese with pesto and serve on crackers or crispbread, on wholegrain toast or to fill a wholemeal pitta pocket. You could also try stirring this into pasta or using it as a filling for cannelloni, topped with tomato ragout then oven-baked.

PREPARATION TIME: less than 10 minutes
COOKING TIME: less than 10 minutes
SERVES 2–4

2 Tbsp pine nuts
½ Tbsp grated Parmesan cheese
Small bunch of fresh basil
2 tsp extra virgin olive oil
500 g (1 lb 2 oz) low-fat natural cottage cheese
Freshly ground black pepper

1 Place the pine nuts in a dry frying pan and place over a medium-high heat for about 6 minutes until they become aromatic and golden. Watch them closely as the nuts burn easily. Set aside on a plate to cool.

2 Once cool, roughly chop the pine nuts and place in a bowl, along with the Parmesan, torn basil, olive oil and cottage cheese. Stir well to combine and season with freshly ground black pepper.

𝒱 = suitable for vegetarians   𝗫 = gluten free   𝗫 = dairy free   ≋ = source of fibre

Cannellini bean salad

This is a really quick dish that uses the best of the ready-made ingredients to be found in the supermarket. It is best prepared in advance and so is the perfect packed lunch.

PREPARATION TIME: less than 10 minutes + chilling time
COOKING TIME: none
SERVES 2

Generous sprig of fresh rosemary
400 g (14 oz) tinned cannellini beans, drained and rinsed
200-g (7-oz) jar of marinated antipasti vegetables, including
    artichoke hearts, peppers and sun-dried tomatoes

Bash the rosemary with the handle of a knife to release the aromatic oils. Place in a bowl with the remaining ingredients and stir well to combine. Refrigerate for at least 2 hours and remove from the fridge 1 hour before serving.

57

Chicken and mango pitta

If you've made roast chicken and have some left-overs to use up, combine the chicken with mango and curry powder for a great pitta filling.

PREPARATION TIME: less than 10 minutes
COOKING TIME: none
SERVES 1

1 roast chicken fillet or around 100 g (3½ oz) of left-over roast chicken
Flesh from ¼ mango, diced
1 spring onion, finely sliced
1 tsp reduced fat mayonnaise
½ Tbsp low-fat natural yoghurt
Good pinch of curry powder

Shred the chicken fillet into bite-sized pieces and combine in a bowl with the mango, spring onion and remaining ingredients. Mix well before serving as a filling for toasted pitta bread or wholegrain sandwiches.

 = heart healthy   = counts towards 5-a-day   = lower fat

Marinated olives

Olives are packed full of monounsaturated fats. These are the fats that help lower unhealthy LDL cholesterol and raise healthy HDL cholesterol, so olives are a great choice for nibbles. Marinating them yourself makes plain olives in brine that bit more interesting and allows you to mix and match the flavours as you like.

PREPARATION TIME: less than 10 minutes
COOKING TIME: none
SERVES 8–10

500 g (1 lb 2 oz) green or black olives (or a mix of both) in brine,
    stone in
Extra virgin olive oil
Selection of flavourings including: garlic, thyme, fresh rosemary,
    herbes de Provence, lemon peel, orange peel, coriander seeds,
    dried chilli peppers and peppercorns

1 Drain the olives and rinse under cold water. To make a number of variations of marinades, place the olives into small jam jars. Add the flavourings of your choice and top up with olive oil. Set aside for at least an hour before serving but these will keep in the fridge for a couple of weeks.

2 Some nice variations include: garlic with lemon rind and herbes de Provence; orange rind with toasted and cracked coriander seeds; dried chilli with cracked peppercorns; rosemary with whole garlic cloves and fennel seeds.

𝒱 = suitable for vegetarians   ✗ = gluten free   ✗ = dairy free   = source of fibre

Orange and coriander barley salad

This salad makes a great packed lunch – just prepare it in the evening and pop it in your lunchbox, ready to grab on your way to work in the morning!

PREPARATION TIME: less than 20 minutes
COOKING TIME: 30–60 minutes
SERVES 2

60 g (2½ oz) pearl barley
½ tsp coriander seeds
1 orange
3 Tbsp chopped coriander

59

1 Boil the barley for 40–45 minutes until tender. Drain and set aside to cool slightly.

2 Pour the coriander seeds in a dry frying pan and place over a medium-high heat until the seeds become aromatic and start to pop. Grind using a pestle and mortar until the seeds have just cracked open, but not to a fine powder.

3 Cut the top and bottom off the orange so it will sit flat on a plate. Using a sharp knife, cut off the peel, removing the white pith as well as the skin. Cut away each segment of orange and then cut each of the segments into three. Place in a bowl and add the barley, ground coriander seeds and freshly chopped coriander. Refrigerate until needed.

❤ = heart healthy   🍎 = counts towards 5-a-day   ✕ = lower fat

Spicy chickpea salad

This is another salad that takes no time at all to make. Prepare it in the evening and take a lunchbox of Middle-eastern flavours to work!

PREPARATION TIME: less than 10 minutes
COOKING TIME: none
SERVES 2

1 heaped Tbsp low-fat natural yoghurt
¼ tsp harissa, or to taste
Good pinch of ground cumin
100 g (3½ oz) cooked chickpeas
2 stalks of celery, including leaves, chopped
1 Tbsp pistachios
1 Tbsp sultanas

60

In a bowl, stir the yoghurt, harissa and cumin together. Stir in the remaining ingredients and refrigerate until needed. Bring to room temperature before serving.

𝒱 = suitable for vegetarians   ✗ = gluten free   ✗ = dairy free   = source of fibre

Summer barley salad

Barley usually takes around 45 minutes to cook but this does depend to some extent on how fresh it is. If the barley has been at the back of the cupboard for a while, it might take a few minutes more but you want the barley to be tender while still retaining a little bite – it will be a similar texture to brown rice when it's cooked.

PREPARATION TIME: less than 10 minutes
COOKING TIME: 30–60 minutes
SERVES 2

60 g (2 oz) pearl barley
1 tsp olive oil
2 baby leeks, sliced
1 small carrot
2 small stalks of celery, including leaves, sliced
3 Tbsp roughly chopped parsley
1 tsp extra virgin olive oil
1 tsp red wine vinegar

61

1 Boil the barley for 40–45 minutes, or until tender. In the meantime, heat the olive oil in a pan and cook the leek for 1–2 minutes to take off the raw edge. Transfer to a bowl and add the carrot, half grated and half cut into paper-thin strips with a potato peeler, celery and parsley.

2 Drain the barley and allow to cool for 5–10 minutes before stirring into the vegetables and dressing with the extra virgin olive oil and red wine vinegar. Refrigerate, in an air-tight container until needed.

♥ = heart healthy 🍎 = counts towards 5-a-day ✕ = lower fat

Bloody Mary salad

Tomatoes, celery, hot pepper and Worcestershire sauce... the basis for a good Bloody Mary, with vodka, of course! These flavours work so well together, here's another way to combine them in a salad you can take to work as a packed lunch – minus the vodka!

PREPARATION TIME: less than 30 minutes
COOKING TIME: none
SERVES 2

125 g (4½ oz) bulgar (cracked) wheat
1 ripe plum tomato, diced
6 cherry tomatoes, halved
4 sun-dried tomatoes in oil, diced
2 stalks of celery, thinly sliced, including leafy tops
½ tsp harissa, or to taste
2 Tbsp chopped flat leaf parsley
Dash of Worcestershire sauce
1–2 Tbsp extra virgin olive oil
Lime juice

1 Place the bulgar wheat in a heat-proof bowl and pour over enough boiling water to cover by 2 cm (¾ in). Set aside for 20 minutes to soften.

2 In the meantime, combine the plum tomato, cherry tomatoes, sun-dried tomatoes and celery in a bowl. Stir in the harissa, parsley and Worcestershire sauce.

3 When the bulgar wheat has softened and swollen, drain off the excess water and stir into the tomato mix. Dress with the olive oil and a good squeeze of lime juice.

$\mathcal{V}$ = suitable for vegetarians   ✗ = gluten free   ✗ = dairy free   = source of fibre

Chickpea and tomato salad

It's usually best to dress salad just as it is about to be served, but it's fine to dress this one ahead of time as it allows the flavours to infuse. Do, however, leave adding the salad leaves to the last minute, especially if you're taking this as a packed lunch, otherwise the salad will be soggy and unappetizing!

PREPARATION TIME: less than 10 minutes

COOKING TIME: none

SERVES 2

100 g (3½ oz) cooked chickpeas

1 plum tomato, diced

10 fresh oregano leaves, or a good pinch of dried oregano

2 tsp extra virgin olive oil

Juice from ¼ lemon

Mixed herb salad (a bag of mixed salad is handy)

63

Combine the chickpeas, tomato and oregano and dress with the olive oil and lemon juice. Refrigerate until needed. Bring to room temperature and add a handful of herb salad leaves before serving.

❤ = heart healthy   🍎🥕 = counts towards 5-a-day   ✗ = lower fat

Carrot and cumin salad

Coriander seeds are often served with carrots since they have a flavour reminiscent of orange – and carrot and orange is definitely a winning combination. Swap the yoghurt in this recipe for a little orange juice or try adding some orange pieces, too, to ring the changes.

PREPARATION TIME: less than 10 minutes
COOKING TIME: none
SERVES 2

½ tsp cumin seeds
½ tsp coriander seeds
2 carrots
1 heaped Tbsp natural yoghurt

1 Heat a small pan and add the cumin and coriander seeds. Toast these for 5–6 minutes until they release their fragrance. Set aside to cool and then crack them open using a pestle and mortar (or a bowl and the end of a rolling pin).

2 Finely grate the carrots – this takes no time at all if it's done in the food processor. Transfer these to a bowl and stir in the seeds and yoghurt. Mix well and refrigerate before serving.

Butter bean and chorizo salad

This dish is ideal for serving as tapas. Tapas is really a selection of small dishes – beans, fish and shellfish, hams, roast vegetables, potatoes and meatballs, for example, that are shared across the table. This is a firm tradition with the Spanish, who tend to eat their main meal of the day at lunch time and have tapas in the evening with a glass of wine.

PREPARATION TIME: less than 10 minutes
COOKING TIME: less than 10 minutes
SERVES 2

1 chorizo sausage or a 10-cm (4-in) piece from a larger chorizo, cut into coins
1 clove of garlic, peeled and crushed
400 g (14 oz) tinned butter beans, drained and rinsed
2 Tbsp chopped flat leaf parsley

65

Place the coins of chorizo in a non-stick frying pan. Bring the pan up to a medium-high heat – heating the chorizo in the pan from cold allows excess oil to melt. Cook the chorizo until crisp on both sides. Drain off the excess oil before adding the garlic and butter beans to the pan. Cook for just long enough to heat through and stir in the flat leaf parsley just before serving.

= heart healthy   = counts towards 5-a-day   X = lower fat

Crab, cucumber and watercress pittas

Crab is a relatively low calorie food and is a good source of protein. It does contain some cholesterol, as do many types of shellfish, but we now know that saturated fat, not dietary cholesterol, has the greatest impact on blood cholesterol levels. The peppery flavour of watercress really complements the mild flavour of crab.

PREPARATION TIME: less than 10 minutes
COOKING TIME: none
SERVES 2

170 g (6 oz) tinned crab meat in brine, drained
1 tsp reduced fat mayonnaise
1 tsp low-fat natural yoghurt
2-cm (¾-in) piece of cucumber, diced
Freshly ground black pepper
Lemon juice
2 wholemeal pitta breads
Handful of watercress

1 Combine the crab meat with the mayonnaise, yoghurt and cucumber and mix well. Season with freshly ground black pepper and a splash of lemon juice.

2 Line the pitta pockets with the watercress and fill with the crab mixture.

66

Fennel and radish salad

Sesame oil is mixed here with rapeseed (canola) oil. Rapeseed is high in monounsaturates but has a less pronounced flavour than olive oil so it makes a good carrier oil for sesame seed oil. This often needs to be combined with a flavourless oil as it has a very powerful nutty flavour and can be overwhelming if used alone.

PREPARATION TIME: less than 10 minutes
COOKING TIME: less than 10 minutes
SERVES 2

1 rounded tsp sesame seeds
1 small or ½ large bulb of fennel
1 bunch of radishes
1 Tbsp golden sultanas
1 Tbsp cashew nuts, roughly chopped
Pinch of Chinese 5-spice powder
½ tsp sesame oil
1 tsp rapeseed oil
Dash of rice vinegar

1 Heat a small frying pan and add the sesame seeds. Dry-fry for 5–6 minutes until golden and aromatic. Set aside on a plate to cool.

2 Cut the fennel and radishes as thinly as possible, using a mandolin if you have one (a food processor or very sharp knife would also do the trick). Combine in a bowl with the sultanas, cashew nuts, 5-spice powder, oils and rice vinegar. Sprinkle with the toasted sesame seeds before serving.

 = heart healthy   = counts towards 5-a-day   = lower fat

Carrot and fennel salad

Cooking carrots increases their GI value so using them raw is the best way to take advantage of their very high beta-carotene content. Adding toasted fennel seeds gives an extra kick of flavour and makes for a nice pitta filling.

PREPARATION TIME: less than 10 minutes
COOKING TIME: none
SERVES 2

1 tsp fennel seeds
2 carrots
1 heaped Tbsp natural yoghurt

1 Heat a small pan and add the fennel seeds. Toast these for 5–6 minutes until they are aromatic, then set aside to cool.

2 Finely grate the carrots – this takes no time at all if it's done in the food processor. Transfer these to a bowl and stir in the fennel seeds and yoghurt. Mix well and refrigerate before serving.

𝒱 = suitable for vegetarians   ✕ = gluten free   ✕ = dairy free   = source of fibre

Spiced pitta chips

Pitta breads are a good choice when it comes to GI and baking them with spices so they crisp up makes a nice change to plain old toasted pitta.

PREPARATION TIME: less than 10 minutes
COOKING TIME: less than 20 minutes
SERVES 4

4 wholegrain pitta breads
½ tsp paprika
½ tsp smoked sweet paprika
½ tsp cumin
½ tsp oregano
1 Tbsp extra virgin olive oil

Preheat the oven to 220° C (425° F/gas mark 7). Cut each of the pitta breads into six. Combine the spices with the olive oil and toss the pitta bread in the flavoured oil. Place on a baking tray and toast in the oven for 10 minutes or until starting to crisp up.

69

♥ = heart healthy   🍎 = counts towards 5-a-day   ✕ = lower fat

Three-bean salad

This traditional-style three-bean salad uses green beans, chickpeas and kidney beans. This combination provides a pleasing mix of colour and texture. But it's really fine to use whatever beans you have handy – butter beans, black-eye beans or haricot beans, for example, but remember that broad beans are the only beans with a high GI value.

PREPARATION TIME: less than 10 minutes

COOKING TIME: less than 30 minutes

SERVES 4

For the dressing:

1 Tbsp extra virgin olive oil

1 Tbsp red wine vinegar

1 shallot, finely chopped

1 clove of garlic, crushed

1 Tbsp chopped fresh tarragon

1 Tbsp chopped fresh parsley

For the salad:

200 g (7 oz) green beans

200 g (7 oz) tinned chickpeas, drained and rinsed

200 g (7 oz) tinned kidney beans, drained and rinsed

1 Prepare the dressing by combining all the ingredients for the dressing in a jam jar, sealing and shaking well together. Set aside.

2 Trim the green beans and cut into 3-cm (1½-in) pieces. Boil for 3 minutes, then add the chickpeas and kidney beans and cook for a further minute to heat through. Drain, transfer to a bowl and toss with the dressing. Serve warm or at room temperature.

70

$\mathcal{V}$ = suitable for vegetarians   X = gluten free   X = dairy free   = source of fibre

Tuna pâté

Tuna sandwiches are another common lunchtime fixture so give them a bit of oomph every so often with vegetables and Tabasco. Using a combination of reduced fat mayonnaise and low-fat natural yoghurt lowers the fat and calorie content.

PREPARATION TIME: less than 10 minutes

COOKING TIME: none

SERVES 4

1 stalk of celery, roughly chopped
2 spring onions
½ small red pepper, roughly chopped
1 level Tbsp reduced fat mayonnaise
1 level Tbsp low-fat natural yoghurt
370 g (13 oz) tinned tuna in brine, drained
Few drops Tabasco sauce

71

1 Place the celery, spring onions and red pepper into the food processor and blitz until finely chopped. Add the mayonnaise, yoghurt and tuna and blitz again until all the ingredients are combined.

2 Serve with wholegrain crackers, rye crispbread or as a filling for wholegrain sandwiches or pitta, with plenty of green salad.

vegetarian dishes

Leek and asparagus risotto

Risotto is traditionally made with arborio or carnaroli rice but these both have high GI values. Using brown rice instead means the dish provides more fibre, is more satisfying and has a lower GI value.

PREPARATION TIME: less than 10 minutes
COOKING TIME: 1 hour or more
SERVES 2

10 g (⅓ oz) butter
1 tsp olive oil
150 g (5½ oz) leek, sliced
125 g (4½ oz) brown rice
125 ml (4 fl oz) white wine
½ tsp thyme
Good pinch of saffron
500–700 ml (1–1½ pints) well-flavoured vegetable stock
2 cloves of garlic, peeled
10 asparagus spears, cut into 2.5-cm (1-in) pieces
25 g (1 oz) grated Parmesan
Balsamic vinegar, to serve

1 Preheat the oven to 180° C (350° F/gas mark 4). Melt the butter and oil together in a large pan and add the leeks. Cook for 4–5 minutes to soften slightly, then stir in the rice. Mix well so all the grains of rice are coated in oil and cook for another 2 minutes. Increase the heat and pour in the wine, allowing this to reduce by half in volume. Add the thyme and saffron, then the stock and transfer to an oven-proof dish.

2 Peel the cloves of garlic but don't crush or chop them – instead, flatten them slightly with the back of a knife and dot around in the rice. Place the dish high in the oven and bake for 45 minutes. Check after the first 20 minutes and add a little more stock if necessary, then again after another 20 minutes. After 45 minutes, add the asparagus, and return to the oven for 5 minutes. Add the Parmesan and return to the oven, with the heat turned off, for a further 5 minutes. Serve with a dash of balsamic vinegar.

$\mathcal{V}$ = suitable for vegetarians   X = gluten free   X = dairy free   = source of fibre

Open mushroom lasagne

This mushroom sauce could be stirred into pasta shapes but layering it with warm sheets of lasagne is an attractive presentation. While pasta is low GI and a good choice, this sauce uses cream, so is definitely an occasional, not an everyday, dish.

PREPARATION TIME: less than 20 minutes

COOKING TIME: less than 30 minutes

SERVES 2

10 g (⅓ oz) dried mixed mushrooms or porcini
1 tsp olive oil
1 small onion, peeled and sliced
2 cloves of garlic, peeled and crushed
1 stalk of celery, finely chopped
260 g (9 oz) button mushrooms, sliced
50 ml (2 fl oz) red wine
1 Tbsp double cream
2 Tbsp fresh parsley
4 sheets of lasagne, either fresh or soaked, following package instructions

75

1 Place the dried mushrooms in a bowl and pour over 125 ml (4 fl oz) boiling water. Set aside to soak for 20 minutes.

2 Heat the oil in a non-stick frying pan and cook the onion for 3 minutes to soften slightly. Add the garlic and celery and cook for a further 5 minutes, without browning, then add the fresh mushrooms.

3 Drain the dried mushrooms, reserving the soaking water, and chop these roughly, then add to the pan. Increase the heat and pour in the wine, along with the mushroom soaking water. Bring to the boil and simmer for 15–20 minutes or until the volume has reduced to about 2 tablespoons.

4 Stir in the cream and parsley. Cook the lasagne sheets following package instructions. Place spoonfuls of mushroom sauce onto 2 plates, cover with a sheet of lasagne and repeat, finishing with a final layer of mushroom sauce. Sprinkle with more freshly chopped parsley before serving.

♥ = heart healthy   = counts towards 5-a-day   ✕ = lower fat

Mushroom burger with feta and pine nuts

Large field mushrooms have a lovely firm texture and a robust, earthy flavour that stands up well to the saltiness of feta cheese. If you're trying to cut down on your red meat, try this giant mushroom sandwich – even the most confirmed carnivores should find this satisfying!

PREPARATION TIME: less than 10 minutes
COOKING TIME: less than 30 minutes
SERVES 2

2 large portobello mushrooms
1 tsp extra virgin olive oil
2 part-baked ciabatta rolls
2 Tbsp pine nuts
1 clove of garlic, peeled and crushed
100 g (3½ oz) feta cheese
2 Tbsp chopped flat leaf parsley

1 Preheat the oven to 200° C (400° F/gas mark 6). Brush the mushrooms lightly with the olive oil and place on a baking tray in the bottom half of the oven for 10 minutes.

2 After this time, place the ciabatta rolls on the top shelf of the oven and cook for a further 8–10 minutes, as directed on the package.

3 Two minutes before the end of the cooking time, sprinkle the pine nuts over another baking tray and toast in the oven. In the meantime, stir the garlic into the feta cheese, along with the parsley. Mix well together, mashing lightly with the back of a fork, adding ½ tablespoon of water to loosen slightly if necessary. Roughly chop the toasted pine nuts and add these to the feta mix.

4 Split the ciabatta rolls open and spread with the feta mixture, then top with the mushrooms.

v = suitable for vegetarians   = gluten free   = dairy free   = source of fibre

Sweet potato curry

This is a lovely aromatic curry which is quite mild in flavour, thanks to the coconut milk. Add an extra chilli or two if you prefer more kick and feel free to add as many veggies to this as you wish – spinach, pak choi, broccoli, baby sweetcorn or sugar snap peas would all go well and add even more colour!

PREPARATION TIME: less than 20 minutes
COOKING TIME: less than 30 minutes
SERVES 3–4

77

For the curry paste:
2 tsp vegetable oil
1 small bunch of coriander, leaves and stalks
2 small hot chillis
2 stalks of lemongrass, tough outer leaves removed
2.5-cm (1-in) piece of ginger, peeled and roughly chopped
2 cloves of garlic, peeled and roughly chopped
½ tsp ground coriander
Juice of ½ lime

For the sweet potato mix:
1 onion, peeled and sliced
2 large sweet potatoes, peeled and cut into 4-cm (1½-in) chunks
400 ml (14 fl oz) of reduced fat coconut milk
4 lime leaves
400 g (14 oz) tinned chickpeas, drained and rinsed

1 Start by preparing the curry paste. Place all the ingredients for the paste in the bowl of the food processor and pulse until well combined.

2 Heat a non-stick frying pan and add the paste. Cook over a medium-high heat until the paste becomes aromatic and sizzles. Add the onion and the sweet potatoes. Stir around to coat in the paste, then pour in the coconut milk and add the lime leaves. Bring to the boil and simmer, uncovered, for 20 minutes. Add the chickpeas and cook for a further 10 minutes.

♥ = heart healthy   🍎 = counts towards 5-a-day   ✗ = lower fat

Roast aubergine pesto with pasta and cherry tomatoes

There are a lot of good pestos available in the supermarkets these days but it's still nice to make your own every so often. This version doesn't use any cheese but it's fine to add grated Parmesan or pecorino as you wish.

PREPARATION TIME: less than 10 minutes
COOKING TIME: less than 30 minutes
SERVES 3

1 small aubergine
Punnet of cherry tomatoes
1 Tbsp pine nuts
100 g (3½ oz) pasta
1 Tbsp extra virgin olive oil
1 small bunch of basil
8 black or green olives, or a mix of both

1 Preheat the oven to 200° C (400° F/gas mark 6). Pierce the aubergine all over with a fork and place high in the oven, directly on the oven rack. Place the cherry tomatoes on a baking tray, and, after 10 minutes, place in the oven to join the aubergine and roast for a further 20 minutes.

2 Scatter the pine nuts over a baking tray and place in the oven for the last couple of minutes of cooking time. Don't leave these more than 3 or 4 minutes, as they burn easily. At this stage, the aubergine should be soft and almost charred, the tomatoes soft and the pine nuts golden and aromatic.

3 In the meantime, bring a large pan of water to the boil and boil the pasta for 8–12 minutes, depending on the type of pasta (follow package directions).

4 When the aubergine is cool enough to handle, cut in half lengthways and scoop out the insides with a spoon. Place in the bowl of the food processor, along with the olive oil, torn basil, pine nuts and olives. Blitz until smooth – add a spoonful or two of water if needed to loosen the mix.

5 Drain the pasta and return it to the warm pan. Stir in the aubergine pesto and roast cherry tomatoes.

78

V = suitable for vegetarians   ✗ = gluten free   ✗ = dairy free   = source of fibre

Polenta with roast vegetables

Polenta or cornmeal has a medium GI value but this is a case where the overall GI of the meal is lowered by adding low GI foods. Low GI vegetables, butter and cheese all combine to not only lower the GI but provide a really tasty meal!

PREPARATION TIME: less than 10 minutes
COOKING TIME: less than 30 minutes
SERVES 2–3

1 red onion, peeled and quartered
1 white onion, peeled and quartered
2 ripe plum tomatoes, quartered
1 small courgette, cut into 4-cm (1½-in) pieces
½ aubergine, cut into 4-cm (1½-in) pieces
4 cloves of garlic, unpeeled
½ Tbsp chilli oil
½ Tbsp extra virgin olive oil
½ teacup of instant polenta
10 g (⅓ oz) butter
1 Tbsp grated Parmesan cheese
½ tsp olive oil

79

1 Preheat the oven to 200° C (400° F/gas mark 6). Place the onions, tomatoes, courgette and aubergine on a baking tray and tuck the unpeeled garlic cloves in and around the vegetables. Drizzle with the oils and roast for about 15 minutes.

2 In the meantime, place the polenta in a small pan and add 1½ teacups of water. Bring to the boil and simmer for 3 minutes, or as directed on the package. Be careful not to get too close – boiling polenta can erupt like a volcano! Remove from the heat and stir in the butter and grated Parmesan.

3 Brush a 20-cm (8-in) baking tin with the olive oil and spread over the polenta to cover the base. Place in the oven along with the vegetables and bake for 15 minutes, lowering the oven temperature to 180° C (350° F/gas mark 4).

4 After this time, the vegetables will be soft and just beginning to char at the edges. Squeeze the soft roast garlic cloves from their skins and spread over the polenta like butter over bread. Serve the polenta in slices with roast veggies on the side.

♥ = heart healthy   🍎 = counts towards 5-a-day   ✕ = lower fat

Wholegrain pizza

Commercially-made pizza is, unfortunately, not up there on the list of healthiest foods. But just because you've decided to eat more healthily doesn't mean that pizza has to be off the menu – just swap that white flour base for a wholemeal version and be sure to add plenty of vegetable toppings. Using strongly-flavoured cheese also means you can add less, so this is an opportunity to lower the fat content.

PREPARATION TIME: less than 20 minutes
COOKING TIME: less than 30 minutes
EACH PIZZA SERVES 2

For the pizza base:
350 g (12½ oz) strong wholemeal flour
200 g (7 oz) strong white flour
1 sachet (7 g/¼ oz) fast acting yeast
1½ tsp salt
2 tsp granulated sugar
4 Tbsp extra virgin olive oil
350–400 ml (12–14 fl oz) hand-hot water

For the tomato sauce:
1 tsp olive oil
1 onion, peeled and chopped
1 stalk of celery, diced
1 small carrot, diced
2 cloves of garlic, peeled and crushed
400 g (14 oz) tinned chopped tomatoes
½ Tbsp tomato purée

1 Start by making the pizza base. Sieve the flours into a large bowl and sprinkle over the yeast. Stir in the salt and sugar and make a well in the centre of the ingredients. Pour in the oil and half the water and, using one hand, begin to incorporate the dry ingredients into the liquid. Add more water as needed to form a dough that is firm but not sticky.

2 Flour a work surface and turn the dough out. Knead the dough for 12 minutes: work the dough by stretching it gently and folding it over on itself. It will gradually become smoother and more elastic. Place in an oiled bowl, cover and set aside in a warm place for 10 minutes.

𝒱 = suitable for vegetarians   ✕ = gluten free   ✕ = dairy free   = source of fibre

3 Split the dough into four pieces and work each of these gently into a ball. Place in the refrigerator for 15 minutes, then roll each ball of dough out to form a pizza base. These are now ready to top and bake for 15–20 minutes at 200° C (400° F/gas mark 6).

4 To prepare the tomato sauce, heat the olive oil and add the onion, celery and carrot. Cook over a medium-high heat for 2 minutes, then reduce the heat, cover and allow to sweat for 8 minutes, stirring occasionally. Add the crushed garlic and cook for a further 3 minutes. Pour in the tomatoes and tomato purée, cover and simmer for 30 minutes. After this time, liquidize using either the blender attachment of the food processor or a hand-held immersion blender.

Some topping suggestions

Roast pepper and pesto
Spread 1 heaped tablespoon of tomato sauce over the base and top with strips of roasted red and yellow peppers, drizzle with spoonfuls of pesto and top with Parmesan cheese.

Tomato and mascarpone
Spread 1 heaped tablespoon of tomato sauce over the base and top with slices of plum tomato, halved cherry tomatoes, chopped sun-dried tomatoes and small spoonfuls of mascarpone cheese. Top with torn basil leaves just before serving.

Ricotta and spinach
Spread 1 heaped tablespoon of tomato sauce over the base and top with thawed and drained spinach and spoonfuls of ricotta cheese. Grate with fresh nutmeg before baking.

Artichoke and goat's cheese
Spread 1 heaped tablespoon of tomato sauce over the base and top with artichoke hearts, black and green olives and slices of goat's cheese.

♥ = heart healthy   = counts towards 5-a-day   ✗ = lower fat

Garlic, onion and chive tart

Pastry made using only wholemeal flour tends to be difficult to work with and tastes too heavy. So, using half plain and half wholemeal makes for a lighter pastry that still provides some valuable dietary fibre.

PREPARATION TIME: less than 20 minutes

COOKING TIME: 1 hour or more

SERVES 6

For the pastry:
100 g (3½ oz) wholemeal flour
100 g (3½ oz) plain flour
100 g (3½ oz) block vegetable
  margarine
Ice cold water

For the topping:
5 red onions, peeled and quartered
5 cloves of garlic, unpeeled
20 g (¾ oz) butter
300 ml (10½ fl oz) semi-skimmed milk
20 g (¾ oz) plain flour
150 ml (5 fl oz) reduced fat crème fraîche
Chives
Salt and freshly ground black pepper

1 Start by preparing the pastry. Sieve the flours into a large bowl and transfer into the bowl of a food processor. Cut the margarine into cubes and add to the processor bowl. Pulse until the mixture resembles breadcrumbs. Add in ice-cold water, 1 tablespoon at a time, until the dough starts to come together. Tip back into the bowl and work the dough lightly until it all comes together and forms a ball. Flour the work surface, tip out the dough and press into a rough circle about 2 cm (¾ in) thick. Set on a plate, cover with cling-film and refrigerate for 20 minutes. After this time, preheat the oven to 200° C (400° F/gas mark 6).

2 On a floured work surface, roll out the pastry and use to line a 28-cm (11-in) flan tin. Place a sheet of greaseproof paper over the pastry and cover with baking beans or dry peas, and bake blind for 15 minutes. Remove the beans and paper and bake for another 5 minutes to give the pastry some colour.

3 While the pastry is baking, place the onions on a baking tray, tucking the unpeeled garlic cloves in and around the onion pieces. Place high in the oven and roast for 20 minutes until softened but not charred.

4 In the meantime, prepare the topping: place the butter, milk and flour in a small saucepan and bring to the boil, whisking continuously. Simmer for 3 minutes, then remove from the heat and stir in the crème fraîche.

82

𝒱 = suitable for vegetarians   ✗ = gluten free   ✗ = dairy free   = source of fibre

5 Spoon the roast onions into the pastry shell. Squeeze the roast garlic out of their skins and whisk into the sauce mix. Pour over the onions and then scatter with chopped chives. Bake for 20 minutes.

Quick vegetable satay

Here's a fabulous way towards your 5-a-day! This satay is packed with crisp vegetables while the peanut and chilli sauce adds a bit of interest. Serve with boiled brown or basmati rice or pack into wholemeal pitta breads.

PREPARATION TIME: less than 10 minutes

COOKING TIME: less than 30 minutes

SERVES 3–4

83

For the sauce:
1 Tbsp sweet chilli sauce
1 Tbsp soy sauce
1 Tbsp peanut butter
Juice of 1 lime
1 Tbsp water

For the vegetables:
1 tsp vegetable oil
1 onion, peeled and sliced
2 cloves of garlic, peeled and crushed
1 red pepper, cut into strips
1 yellow pepper, cut into strips
8 florets of broccoli
8 florets of cauliflower
100 g (3½ oz) baby spinach leaves

1 Start by making the sauce. In a small bowl, combine all the ingredients for the sauce and mix well.

2 To prepare the vegetables, heat the oil in a non-stick frying pan and cook the onion and garlic gently for 4 minutes. Add the pepper strips and cook for a further 4 minutes. Turn up the heat and add 2 tablespoons of water to the pan. Add the broccoli and cauliflower florets and cook for a further 4 minutes. Pour in the sauce and bring to a simmer. Add the spinach and cook for a final 2–3 minutes, to wilt the spinach leaves.

♥ = heart healthy   🍎 = counts towards 5-a-day   ✗ = lower fat

Roast artichokes and tomatoes with feta

Peeling and preparing fresh globe artichokes is just too much of a challenge for many of us, so it's very handy that they are available canned in most supermarkets! These are great drizzled with good olive oil on a slice of wholegrain bread or on top of a pizza, or make a more substantial dish by roasting them and topping with salty feta cheese.

PREPARATION TIME: less than 10 minutes
COOKING TIME: less than 30 minutes
SERVES 2

400 g (14 oz) tinned artichoke hearts, drained and rinsed
4 ripe plum tomatoes, halved
½ Tbsp extra virgin olive oil
100 g (3½ oz) feta cheese
10 black olives, halved
Good squeeze of lemon juice
Toasted multi-grain baguette, to serve

Preheat the oven to 200° C (400° F/gas mark 6). Place the artichoke hearts on a baking tray with the tomatoes. Drizzle with the olive oil and roast in the oven for 25–30 minutes. Transfer to a serving plate and, while still warm, crumble over the feta, olives and a good squeeze of lemon juice. Serve with thick slices of toasted multi-grain baguette.

84

$\mathcal{V}$ = suitable for vegetarians ✗ = gluten free ✗ = dairy free = source of fibre

Papardelle with courgette ribbons

Steaming vegetables over boiling pasta is both time- and energy-efficient. Steaming also helps retain vitamins as water-soluble vitamins (B and C) can be destroyed during the boiling process.

PREPARATION TIME: less than 10 minutes
COOKING TIME: less than 10 minutes
SERVES 2

100 g (3½ oz) papardelle or other pasta
1 medium-sized courgette
2 tsp lower fat Greek yoghurt
2 tsp pesto
Zest and juice of ½ lemon
½ Tbsp hazelnuts, roughly chopped

85

1 Bring a large pan of water (one with a steamer bowl, if possible) to the boil and boil the pasta for 8 minutes, or according to package directions.

2 In the meantime, use a potato peeler to cut the courgette into long, thin ribbons. Place these into the steamer attachment, a sieve or colander, and place over the pan of boiling pasta to steam for 5–6 minutes.

3 Drain the pasta and courgette slices and return them to the warm pan. Stir in the Greek yoghurt, pesto, lemon zest and a good squeeze of lemon juice and top with the hazelnuts before serving.

= heart healthy　　= counts towards 5-a-day　　= lower fat

Pasta with roast peppers, pine nuts and cottage cheese

When peppers are in season and inexpensive, it's a good idea to buy plenty and roast them in a large roasting tin. The roast pepper strips can be stored in individual portions, wrapped in cling-film and frozen. Anytime you haven't had a chance to buy fresh veggies or need dinner in a hurry, just defrost these in the microwave for 1–2 minutes before adding to your favourite pasta dish.

PREPARATION TIME: less than 10 minutes
COOKING TIME: less than 30 minutes
SERVES 2

1 red pepper, cut into thick strips
1 yellow pepper, cut into thick strips
½ Tbsp extra virgin olive oil
2 Tbsp pine nuts
100 g (3½ oz) pasta
2 Tbsp cottage cheese
1 level Tbsp tapenade (green or black olive paste)
Fresh oregano leaves (about 15)

1 Preheat the oven to 200° C (400° F/gas mark 6). Place the peppers on a baking tray and toss with the olive oil. Place high in the oven for 25–30 minutes, until just beginning to char.

2 Scatter the pine nuts over a separate baking tray and toast in the oven during the last 1–2 minutes of cooking time.

3 In the meantime, boil the pasta for 8–12 minutes, as directed on the package. In a bowl, mix the cottage cheese and tapenade together. Drain the pasta and return it to the pan. Stir in the cheese mix, peppers and top with toasted pine nuts. Sprinkle over fresh oregano leaves before serving.

$\mathcal{V}$ = suitable for vegetarians   ✗ = gluten free   ✗ = dairy free   = source of fibre

Pasta primavera

As the name suggests, this is the perfect dish for spring but the vegetables used can be varied to suit what's in season or what you have in the fridge!

PREPARATION TIME: less than 10 minutes
COOKING TIME: less than 30 minutes
SERVES 2

100 g (3½ oz) pasta
100 g (3½ oz) peas
100 g (3½ oz) sliced green beans
10 asparagus spears
6 small florets of broccoli
100 g (3½ oz) baby spinach leaves
2 Tbsp reduced fat crème fraîche
2 Tbsp chopped fresh mint
2 Tbsp chopped fresh flat leaf parsley
Freshly ground black pepper

Using a steamer saucepan, boil the pasta for 8–12 minutes, as directed on the package. Place the peas, beans, asparagus and broccoli in the steamer over the pasta for 6 minutes of the cooking time. Drain the pasta and return it to the pan. Place over a very low heat and stir in the steamed vegetables as well as the spinach and crème fraîche. Allow the spinach to wilt before stirring in the chopped herbs and seasoning with freshly ground black pepper.

❤ = heart healthy   🍎 = counts towards 5-a-day   ✕ = lower fat

Pasta with rocket, olives, capers and Parmesan

Here is another super-quick mid-week supper. Dress up pasta with peppery rocket, salty olives and cheese, and dinner is ready in less than 10 minutes!

PREPARATION TIME: less than 10 minutes
COOKING TIME: less than 30 minutes
SERVES 2

100 g (3½ oz) pasta
50 g (2 oz) bag of rocket
10 black olives
2 tsp capers, drained and rinsed if preferred
Parmesan cheese
1 Tbsp extra virgin olive oil
Good squeeze of lemon

88

Boil the pasta for 8–12 minutes, as directed on the package. Drain and return it to the warm pan. Stir in the rocket and allow to wilt very slightly. Transfer to serving plates and scatter over the olives, capers and shavings of Parmesan. Drizzle with the olive oil and a good squeeze of lemon juice.

Noodles with greens and chilli dressing

This dish takes just a few minutes to prepare so it's ideal for a quick mid-week supper. Make things even quicker by using a bag of ready-prepared vegetables from the supermarket.

PREPARATION TIME: less than 10 minutes

COOKING TIME: less than 10 minutes

SERVES 2

For the dressing:
2-cm (¾-in) piece of ginger,
    peeled and grated
1 red chilli, finely sliced
1 tsp sesame oil
½ tsp rice vinegar
1 tsp soy sauce

For the noodles:
2 blocks of egg noodles
150 g (5½ oz) mange-touts
2 pak choi, sliced

89

1 To make the dressing, mix the ginger, chilli (leave some of the seeds in if you prefer a bit more heat) and the remaining ingredients for the dressing in a small bowl. Set aside.

2 Boil the noodles for 4–5 minutes, as directed on the package. During the last 2 minutes of cooking time, add the mange-touts and the whites of the pak choi to the noodles. Add the chopped pak choi greens for the last minute of cooking time. Drain into a bowl and toss with the dressing.

♥ = heart healthy   = counts towards 5-a-day   ✕ = lower fat

Puttanesca pasta

This pasta sauce takes minutes to prepare – by the time the pasta is ready, the sauce is ready to go too. Make things even quicker by using fresh, not dried, pasta and your whole meal will be ready in less than 5 minutes! That's fast food for you!

PREPARATION TIME: less than 10 minutes
COOKING TIME: less than 10 minutes
SERVES 2

100 g (3½ oz) spaghetti
1 Tbsp extra virgin olive oil
4 ripe plum tomatoes, roughly chopped
2 cloves of garlic, peeled and chopped
2 tsp capers
16 black or green olives, or a mix of both

90

1 Bring a large pan of water to the boil and boil the spaghetti for 8 minutes, or according to package directions.

2 Meanwhile, heat the olive oil in a wide pan and, keeping the heat high, add the tomatoes and garlic. Cook for 3–4 minutes, until the tomatoes have softened, then add the capers and olives. Allow to just heat through and use to top the cooked spaghetti.

Stuffed mushrooms with granary pesto breadcrumbs

In too many restaurants, stuffed mushrooms means deep-fried, breadcrumbed balls of cream cheese and just a hint of a mushroom! Forget that! Top giant field mushrooms with pesto, Gruyère and breadcrumbs (or use polenta for a gluten-free option) and serve with salad for a light lunch or inside a toasted wholegrain roll for supper.

PREPARATION TIME: less than 10 minutes

COOKING TIME: less than 30 minutes

SERVES 2

2 large portobello mushrooms
1 slice of granary bread (a slightly stale heel is fine)
1 heaped tsp of your favourite pesto
30 g (1 oz) Gruyère cheese, grated
Mixed salad, to serve

91

1 Preheat the oven to 180° C (350° F/gas mark 4). Place the mushrooms on a baking tray and bake for 5 minutes.

2 During this time, grate the bread into chunky breadcrumbs and mix in the pesto and grated cheese. Remove the mushrooms from the oven and top with the breadcrumb mix. Return to the oven for 15 minutes and serve with a mixed salad.

♥ = heart healthy   = counts towards 5-a-day   ✕ = lower fat

Baked sweet potato frittata

If you prefer, you could cook this frittata in an omelette pan on the hob instead of baking it, just as you would cook a Spanish omelette or tortilla. Either way, it makes a lovely light lunch with a green salad. Or, if you're cooking for friends, multiply up the ingredients, cook it in a pan, and serve, cut it into wedges, as part of a tapas platter.

PREPARATION TIME: less than 10 minutes
COOKING TIME: 30–60 minutes
SERVES 2

1 sweet potato (around 250 g/9 oz), peeled
1 egg
50 ml (2 fl oz) double cream
30 ml (1 fl oz) milk
Grating of nutmeg
1 Tbsp chopped chives
Salt and freshly ground black pepper

1 Preheat the oven to 190° C (375° F/gas mark 5). Slice the sweet potato into 2–3 mm (⅛ in) thick slices, on the diagonal. Par boil for 4 minutes.

2 In a small bowl, mix together the egg, cream, milk, nutmeg and chives and season well with salt and pepper. Beat lightly to break up the egg.

3 Lightly grease two 8-cm (3-in) pudding basins with vegetable oil or cooking spray. Use the sweet potato slices to fill the basins and pour over the egg mix. Place on a baking tray towards the top of the oven and bake for 30 minutes.

$\mathcal{V}$ = suitable for vegetarians ✕ = gluten free ✕ = dairy free 🌾 = source of fibre

Falafels with herb yoghurt

Falafels are usually deep-fried but it seems such a shame to turn healthy chickpeas into a no-go area just by the cooking method. Instead, add just a little olive oil to the mix and bake them instead. Serve warm, tucked inside toasted wholemeal pitta bread.

PREPARATION TIME: less than 10 minutes + chilling time

COOKING TIME: less than 30 minutes

*

SERVES 2–3

For the falafels:

2 cloves of garlic, peeled

400 g (14 oz) tinned chickpeas, rinsed and drained

½ tsp cumin

½ tsp ground coriander

Pinch of baking soda

1 Tbsp buckwheat flour

½ Tbsp extra virgin olive oil

Good pinch of salt

1 tsp olive oil

For the herb yoghurt:

2 Tbsp parsley, finely chopped

2 Tbsp mint, finely chopped

2 Tbsp coriander, finely chopped

1 clove of garlic, peeled and crushed

1 level tsp paprika

4 Tbsp low-fat natural yoghurt

Salad or wholemeal pitta bread, to serve

93

1 Start by making the falafels. Place the garlic in the bowl of the food processor and pulse to roughly chop. Add the rest of the falafel ingredients, along with 1 tablespoon of water, and blitz until combined. Shape the mix into short fat sausages and refrigerate for 30 minutes.

2 Preheat the oven to 200° C (400° F/gas mark 6). Place the falafels on a baking tray and brush lightly with the olive oil. Bake for 15 minutes, turning once.

3 In the meantime, prepare the herb yoghurt. Stir the herbs, garlic and paprika into the yoghurt and refrigerate until needed. Serve the falafels with the yoghurt dressing, along with a salad or in pitta bread.

* gluten free, unless served with wholemeal pitta bread

= heart healthy   = counts towards 5-a-day   = lower fat

Halloumi with caper and harissa dressings

Halloumi is a very unusual Greek cheese in that it is best eaten cooked. It can be dredged in flour and fried in olive oil but it's every bit as good grilled. It's very salty, though, so a little goes a long way and you won't need to add any salt at all to the dressings. Serve with a salad or in a wholemeal pitta bread.

PREPARATION TIME: less than 10 minutes
COOKING TIME: less than 30 minutes
SERVES 2–3

250 g (9 oz) halloumi cheese

94

For the caper dressing:
1 Tbsp extra virgin olive oil
Zest and juice ¼ lemon
2 tsp capers
Small bunch of flat leaf parsley,
  chopped

For the harissa dressing:
2 Tbsp lower fat Greek yogurt
½–1 tsp harissa, to taste
Pinch of cumin
Small bunch of chopped fresh mint

1 Cut the halloumi into slices about 1 cm (½ in) thick. Place on a grill rack and place under a preheated grill. Grill for 10–12 minutes, turning occasionally, until golden brown in places.

2 In the meantime, make the two dressings by combining the ingredients for the respective dressings in separate bowls. Serve the grilled halloumi with the dressings.

𝒱 = suitable for vegetarians ✗ = gluten free ✗ = dairy free = source of fibre

Stuffed aubergine

This is another dish that will satisfy even the most confirmed carnivores as the aubergine is substantial and filling. Dried fruit adds a touch of sweetness to this bulgar stuffing, while preserved lemons add a sour kick.

PREPARATION TIME: less than 10 minutes + soaking time

COOKING TIME: 30–60 minutes

SERVES 2

For the filling:

1 small aubergine

75 g (2½ oz) bulgar wheat

50 g (2 oz) dried apricots, chopped

50 g (2 oz) sultanas

2 preserved lemons, chopped

1 Tbsp extra virgin olive oil

For the dressing:

1 dsp tahini

1 Tbsp extra virgin olive oil

Good squeeze of lemon juice

1 Tbsp water

Tbsp each of chopped flat leaf parsley, mint and coriander

1 tsp sesame seeds

Green salad, to serve

1 Preheat the oven to 200° C (400° F/gas mark 6). Cut the aubergine in half lengthways, then cut diagonal scores through the flesh, making diamond shapes. Place on a baking tray and bake for 20 minutes.

2 In the meantime, place the bulgar wheat in a heat-proof bowl and pour in enough boiling water to cover by 2 cm (¾ in). Set aside for 15 minutes to soften and swell.

3 After this time, drain any excess water from the bulgar wheat and stir in the dried apricots, sultanas, preserved lemon and olive oil. Set aside.

4 Remove the aubergine from the oven and scoop out the flesh with a spoon. Mix this into the bulgar and then use to fill the aubergine shell. Return to the oven, lower the temperature to 180° C (350° F/gas mark 4) and bake for a further 10 minutes.

5 During this time, make a quick dressing by combining all the dressing ingredients in a small bowl. Top the aubergine with sesame seeds and drizzle over the dressing before serving with a green salad.

♥ = heart healthy　🍎 = counts towards 5-a-day　✕ = lower fat

meat

6

Wholegrain paella

Paella is usually made with high GI white paella rice but using brown rice instead lowers the GI of the dish and adds extra fibre. It means the cooking time is longer but, unlike risotto, paella doesn't require your constant attention. This dish is a great way to use up left-overs – use the remains of Sunday's roast, left-over sausages from a weekend breakfast, open a tin of emergency ham or defrost some prawns before throwing them in.

PREPARATION TIME: less than 10 minutes
COOKING TIME: 30–60 minutes
SERVES 2

1 tsp olive oil
1 onion, peeled and chopped
2 cloves of garlic, peeled and crushed
1 teacup of brown rice
1 tsp smoked paprika
1 tsp oregano
750 ml (1¼ pints) vegetable or chicken stock
200 g (7 oz) cooked meat, including diced ham, sliced sausage,
    roast chicken or prawns
1 roast red pepper, cut into strips
100 g (3½ oz) frozen peas

1 Heat the oil in a non-stick frying pan and cook the onion for 5–6 minutes to soften without colouring. Add the garlic, rice, smoked paprika and oregano and mix well. Allow to cook for 2–3 minutes, then add the hot stock. Bring to the boil, then simmer, uncovered, for 20 minutes.

2 After this time, stir in the cooked meat and sliced red pepper. Bring back to the boil and simmer for another 15 minutes. Finally, add the frozen peas and simmer for 5–10 minutes, until the rice is tender. You may need to add more water during the last stages of cooking to prevent sticking.

$\mathcal{V}$ = suitable for vegetarians   ✗ = gluten free   ✗ = dairy free   = source of fibre

Pork with haricot and mustard mash

Some foods were made for each other – strawberries and cream, fish and chips, and pork and apples... and mustard! In this dish, pork steaks are marinated in apple juice before being served with a mustard mash – what could be better on a crisp autumn day!

PREPARATION TIME: less than 10 minutes + marinating time
COOKING TIME: less than 30 minutes
SERVES 2

2 pork spare rib or loin chops
100 ml (3½ fl oz) apple juice
5 allspice berries
400 g (14 oz) tinned haricot beans, drained and rinsed
2 heaped tsp grain mustard, preferably Dijon

1 Start by marinating the pork: pour the apple juice into a glass or ceramic dish and add the allspice berries – crush these open using a pestle and mortar (or the end of a rolling pin and a bowl) but don't grind them to a powder. Add the pork and set aside for 1 hour.

2 Preheat the grill. Remove the chops from the marinade and grill for 15–20 minutes, turning occasionally. Meanwhile, pour the remaining marinade into a saucepan and add the beans. Bring to the boil and boil over a high heat for 5 minutes. Reduce the heat, then simmer for a further 10 minutes. Remove the allspice berries and add the mustard. Mash lightly with a potato masher before serving with the pork steaks.

99

Sweet potato and pork casserole

Sweet potatoes and yam are used a lot in Creole style cookery. This bright and tasty casserole is a great way to bring a bit of sunshine to a rainy day!

PREPARATION TIME: less than 10 minutes
COOKING TIME: 1 hour or more
SERVES 4

1 tsp olive oil
450 g (1 lb) pork pieces
1 onion, peeled and sliced
Small tin of pineapple chunks in juice
1 red chilli, sliced
2 cloves of garlic, peeled and crushed
2 large sweet potatoes, peeled
1 red pepper, cut into thick strips
1 yellow pepper, cut into thick strips
½ tsp of each: dried oregano, dried thyme and paprika
¼ tsp of each: cayenne and celery salt
Juice of 1 lime
1 Tbsp soy sauce

1 Preheat the oven to 160° C (325° F/gas mark 3). Over a medium heat, heat the oil in a casserole dish that's suitable for the hob and the oven. Working in batches, brown the pork pieces all over and set aside on a plate.

2 In the same casserole dish, add the onion and cook for 5–6 minutes to soften without colouring, then pour in a little of the juice from the tin of pineapples. Use this to deglaze the pan, that is, increase the heat and use a wooden spoon to scrape up any tasty brown bits from the bottom of the pan.

3 Add the chilli, leaving the seeds in if you prefer more heat, and garlic, and cook for 2 minutes. Cut the sweet potatoes into 4-cm (1½-in) chunks and add to the pan, along with the peppers and the herbs and spices. Cook over a medium heat for 4 minutes, then return the pork pieces to the pan. Pour in the rest of the pineapple juice, the lime juice and the soy sauce, and place in the oven for 45 minutes. After this time, add the pineapple and cook for a further 10 minutes.

𝒱 = suitable for vegetarians   ✗ = gluten free   ✗ = dairy free   = source of fibre

Rib-eye steaks with butter bean and horseradish mash

Rib-eye is a beautifully tender and flavoursome cut of beef. It is more tender than sirloin and can have a better flavour than fillet steak and is best cooked over high heat for a short period of time. When turning the steaks, remember to use tongs and not a fork as a fork pierces the meat and allows valuable juices to escape.

PREPARATION TIME: less than 10 minutes
COOKING TIME: less than 30 minutes
SERVES 2

400 g (14 oz) tinned butter beans, drained and rinsed
1 Tbsp low-fat natural yoghurt
2 heaped tsp prepared horseradish sauce
2 rib-eye steaks
1 tsp vegetable oil

1 Place the beans in a pan with 1 tablespoon of water. Bring to the boil, then simmer for around 8 minutes. Remove from the heat, add the yoghurt and horseradish, and mash lightly with a potato masher.

2 In the meantime, heat a cast iron griddle pan over a high heat. Lightly brush the steaks with the oil and place them in the centre of the pan. Cook, keeping the heat high for 4 minutes, without moving, then turn over and cook for a further 4–5 minutes. Allow the steaks to rest for a few minutes before serving with the horseradish mash and some grilled tomatoes, if you wish.

101

♥ = heart healthy   = counts towards 5-a-day   ✕ = lower fat

Lamb chops with cannellini and rosemary mash

This recipe uses chops but you could equally well use lamb steaks for an easy weeknight supper. If you're entertaining, try serving the cannellini mash with a roast leg of lamb. Serve with green vegetables such as crisp green beans or broccoli and a redcurrant sauce.

PREPARATION TIME: less than 10 minutes
COOKING TIME: less than 30 minutes
SERVES 2

6 lamb loin chops
1 Tbsp red wine vinegar
1 Tbsp extra virgin olive oil
3 cloves of garlic, peeled and roughly chopped
3 sprigs of rosemary
400 g (14 oz) tinned cannellini beans, drained and rinsed

1 Start by marinating the chops: mix the vinegar and olive oil together in a glass or ceramic dish and add the garlic. Rub this over the lamb and tuck the pieces of garlic in around the meat. Break two of the rosemary sprigs into smaller pieces and tuck these around the meat, too. Refrigerate for 1 hour.

2 Place the beans in a pan with the remaining sprig of rosemary and set aside for 1 hour.

3 Preheat the oven to 190° C (375° F/gas mark 5). Place the chops on a grill rack over a baking tray, leaving the rosemary in the meat but putting the garlic into the beans. Place the baking tray high in the oven and roast for 15–20 minutes.

4 Meanwhile, pour the remaining marinade into the beans, along with 1 tablespoon of water. Bring to the boil and allow to boil over a high heat for 5 minutes. Reduce the heat and simmer for a further 10 minutes. Remove the rosemary and mash lightly with a potato masher before serving with the chops.

102

$\mathcal{V}$ = suitable for vegetarians   ✗ = gluten free   ✗ = dairy free   = source of fibre

Pork with sage and onion stuffing

Stuffing is usually made with breadcrumbs, but it is possible to make stuffing with almost any other carbohydrate base, such as rice, potatoes or polenta. This recipe uses bulgar wheat which gives a nutty texture and flavour to the mix.

PREPARATION TIME: less than 10 minutes

COOKING TIME: 3 hours

SERVES 4

For the stuffing:

100 g (3½ oz) bulgar wheat

1 tsp olive oil

1 small onion, peeled and finely chopped

1 clove of garlic, peeled and crushed

1 tsp dried sage

Scant ½ tsp ground cloves

1 shoulder of pork, around 2 kg (4 lb 6 oz) in weight

1 To make the stuffing, place the bulgar wheat in a heat-proof bowl and pour over enough boiling water to cover by 2 cm (¾ in). Set aside for 15 minutes to soften, then drain.

2 Heat the oil in a small pan and add the onion and garlic. Cook for 5–6 minutes to soften without colouring, then stir in the drained bulgar, sage and cloves. Set the stuffing aside to cool.

3 Preheat the oven to 220° C (425° F/gas mark 7). Open up the pork shoulder and press in the stuffing. Roll up and secure with string. Place on a roasting rack over a tin and place in the oven. Roast for 30 minutes, then turn the oven down to 180° C (350° F/gas mark 4). Cook for 30 minutes per 500 g (1 lb 2 oz), plus 30 minutes in total.

103

♥ = heart healthy   🍎 = counts towards 5-a-day   ✕ = lower fat

Mediterranean lamb casserole

This casserole is bursting with flavours of the Mediterranean – lamb, wine, cumin, mint and that dried chilli paste, harissa. People who follow a traditional Mediterranean diet – plenty of fresh fruit and vegetables, olive oil, nuts and fish, have been found to have lower rates of disease, so serve this dish with griddled vegetables and bulgar wheat for a Mediterranean treat!

PREPARATION TIME: less than 10 minutes

COOKING TIME: more than 1 hour

SERVES 4

2 tsp olive oil
500 g (1 lb 2 oz) lean lamb pieces
1 onion, peeled and sliced
2 cloves of garlic, peeled and crushed
1 dsp plain flour
150 ml (5 fl oz) red wine
1 level tsp cinnamon
½ tsp cumin
½–1 tsp harissa, to taste
400 g (14 oz) tinned chopped tomatoes
1 level Tbsp tomato purée
1 tsp dried mint
2 Tbsp pine nuts
2 Tbsp chopped fresh mint

1 Preheat the oven to 160° C (325° F/gas mark 3). Heat half the oil in a casserole dish and, working in batches, brown the lamb pieces. Set aside on a plate.

2 Add the rest of the oil to the pan and add the onion and garlic. Cook over a medium heat for around 8 minutes, until golden, then stir in the flour. Turn up the heat and add the wine, scraping up any browned pieces from the bottom of the dish. Stir in the cinnamon, cumin and harissa paste, and cook for a couple of minutes, then return the lamb to the dish, along with the tomatoes, tomato purée and mint. Bring to the boil, then transfer to the oven for 1 hour.

3 Heat a small frying pan and dry-fry the pine nuts for around 8 minutes, until toasted and aromatic. Keep watching these as they burn easily. Sprinkle the toasted pine nuts and chopped fresh mint over the casserole before serving.

𝒱 = suitable for vegetarians   ✗ = gluten free   ✗ = dairy free   ≋ = source of fibre

Cassoulet with Gruyère croutons

Cassoulet is a very rustic dish and was originally a peasant dish, since such inexpensive ingredients are used. This is another great way to use up left-over meat or vegetables as almost anything you have in the fridge can be added to make the dish go further.

PREPARATION TIME: less than 10 minutes
COOKING TIME: 1 hour or more
SERVES 4

8 good quality thick sausages
1 onion, peeled and chopped
2 stalks of celery, diced
3 or 4 stalks of fresh thyme
2 heaped tsp paprika
500 g (1 lb 2 oz) carton of passata
400 g (14 oz) tinned haricot beans, drained and rinsed
1 clove of garlic, peeled
4 thick slices of wholegrain baguette
40 g (1½ oz) Gruyère cheese, grated
1 Tbsp grated Parmesan

1 Preheat the oven to 160° C (325° F/gas mark 3). Prick the sausages with a fork or sharp knife and place them in a casserole dish that can be used on the hob and in the oven. Bring up to a medium-high heat and brown the sausages all over. Bringing the heat up gradually allows excess fat to melt and drain off the sausages. Once brown all over, set aside on a plate.

2 Drain off most of the excess fat, then add the onion and celery. Keep the heat high for a couple of minutes, then reduce the heat to low, cover and allow to sweat for 8–10 minutes, stirring occasionally.

3 After this time, add the stalks of fresh thyme, paprika, passata and beans. Stir well, then return the sausages to the pan. Bring back to the boil, half cover with the lid and transfer to the oven for 40 minutes.

4 Cut the garlic clove in half and rub the cut face over the slices of wholegrain baguette. Mix the Gruyère and Parmesan together and sprinkle over the slices. Set these croutons on top of the casserole and cook, uncovered for a further 5–10 minutes, until the cheese is melted and golden.

105

♥ = heart healthy   🍎 = counts towards 5-a-day   ✕ = lower fat

Steak sandwich with tomatoes and horseradish

This is the perfect Friday night supper! It's ready in the blink of an eye and is massively satisfying. Use either the small multi-grain baguettes from the bakery or keep a pack of bake-at-home rolls in the larder for just this kind of meal.

PREPARATION TIME: less than 10 minutes
COOKING TIME: less than 10 minutes
SERVES 2

2 multi-grain demi-baguettes
2 ripe plum tomatoes, halved
300 g (10½ oz) thin steak slices
2 tsp horseradish sauce
1 bag of mixed salad

1 Turn the oven on to a low heat, around 120° C (250° F/gas mark ½) and place the baguettes in the oven to warm through. Or, if using bake-at-home rolls, prepare these following package directions.

2 Heat a cast iron griddle pan over a medium-high heat and add the tomatoes, cut side up. Allow to cook for 4 minutes, then increase the heat and cook the steak slices – these should take only 45 seconds to 1 minute each. Remove to a covered oven-proof plate and keep warm in the oven. Remove the tomatoes to the oven too, when they have softened and cooked down.

3 Cut the baguettes in half lengthways and spread with horseradish sauce. Fill with the steak slices, pouring in any juice from the plate, and top with the tomatoes and mixed salad leaves.

𝒱 = suitable for vegetarians   ✗ = gluten free   ✗ = dairy free   = source of fibre

Giant sandwich with chorizo, roast peppers and rocket

This recipe calls for the short fat chorizo sausages that are often available at the deli counter in supermarkets. If you can't find these, just use pre-sliced chorizo – the type that comes in thin circles and should be found in the chiller cabinet in the supermarket. That type won't need any cooking.

PREPARATION TIME: less than 10 minutes
COOKING TIME: less than 10 minutes
SERVES 2

2 multi-grain demi-baguettes
4 good quality thick sausages
1 red pepper
1 tsp extra virgin olive oil
10-cm (4-in) piece of chorizo
Handful of rocket, rinsed

1 Preheat the grill. Cut the baguettes in half lengthways and place under the grill to warm through.

2 Prick the sausages with a fork and place under the grill. Cut the pepper into quarters, brush lightly with oil and place under the grill. Cook for around 6 minutes, turning occasionally, then slice the piece of chorizo into half lengthways, and in half again, and add to the grill tray. Continue to grill until the sausages are cooked though and the peppers are softened and lightly charred.

3 Pile the cooked sausages, pepper slices and strips of chorizo into the warm baguettes and top with rocket.

Sausage bake

This is the easiest dinner ever. Simply pile sausages, chunks of sweet potato and vegetables into a roasting tray and pop it in the oven for an hour! What comes out is the most delicious meal – soft pieces of sweet potato, beautifully browned sausages and vegetables flavoured with chorizo oil.

PREPARATION TIME: less than 10 minutes
COOKING TIME: 1 hour or more
SERVES 4

2 red onions, peeled and quartered
2 red peppers, quartered
8 good quality thick sausages
2 small chorizo sausages (or about 20 cm/8 in), cut into coins
3 large sweet potatoes, peeled
12 cherry tomatoes
1 level tsp smoked paprika
3 sprigs of fresh rosemary

1 Preheat the oven to 200° C (400° F/gas mark 6). Place the onions and peppers in a large roasting tin. Prick the sausages with a fork and add these to the vegetables, along with the chorizo and sweet potatoes cut into 4-cm (1½-in) chunks. Mix in the cherry tomatoes and sprinkle with smoked paprika. Tuck the sprigs of rosemary in and around the ingredients and toss everything well together.

2 Bake for 10 minutes and give everything another good toss, lower the oven temperature to 180° C (350° F/gas mark 4) and cook for a further 50 minutes.

𝒱 = suitable for vegetarians   ✗ = gluten free   ✗ = dairy free   = source of fibre

Lamb with preserved lemon bulgar

Bulgar is a type of whole wheat grain that has been cracked open and dried. It is prepared – and used – in a similar way to couscous and is often used in Moroccan and Middle Eastern cookery. Herbs, lemon and good olive oil transform what could be a very plain grain into a delicious dish.

PREPARATION TIME: less than 10 minutes + marinating time
COOKING TIME: less than 30 minutes
SERVES 2

For the lamb:
2 lamb leg steaks
Juice of ½ lemon
1 Tbsp extra virgin olive oil
2 cloves of garlic,
   peeled and roughly chopped
1 heaped tsp dried mint

For the bulgar:
100 g (3½ oz) bulgar wheat
2 preserved lemons, finely chopped
2 Tbsp roughly chopped flat leaf parsley
2 Tbsp roughly chopped coriander
2 Tbsp roughly chopped mint
1 Tbsp extra virgin olive oil

109

1 Start by marinating the lamb steaks: mix the lemon juice and olive oil together in a glass or ceramic dish and add the garlic and mint. Rub this over the lamb and tuck the pieces of garlic in around the meat. Refrigerate for at least 1 hour.

2 In the meantime, place the bulgar in a heat-proof bowl and add enough water to cover by 2 cm (¾ in). Set aside for 10–15 minutes to soften and swell.

3 When you're ready to eat, heat a cast iron griddle pan over a high heat. Drain the excess marinade off the lamb steaks and place them in the centre of the pan. Cook, keeping the heat high for 3 minutes, without moving, then turn over and cook for a further 3 minutes. Allow the lamb to rest for a few minutes.

4 Drain the bulgar wheat and add the two preserved lemons, removing the pips, the herbs and olive oil. Serve the lamb on a bed of bulgar wheat.

♥ = heart healthy = counts towards 5-a-day ✗ = lower fat

Chinese 5-spice pork with noodles and pak choi

Chinese 5-spice is a flavouring made from equal parts of ground cinnamon, fennel, star anise, cloves and Szechwan pepper. It is available in most supermarkets and will certainly be available in Asian food shops.

PREPARATION TIME: less than 10 minutes + marinating time

COOKING TIME: less than 30 minutes

SERVES 2

1 tsp sesame oil
1 tsp vegetable oil
1 tsp rice vinegar
½ tsp Chinese 5-spice powder
2-cm (¾-in) piece of ginger, peeled and grated
1 clove of garlic, peeled and crushed
1 star anise, broken into pieces
2 pork leg steaks

2 blocks of egg noodles
2 pak choi, cut into 2.5-cm (1-in) pieces
½ tsp sesame oil

1 Start by marinating the pork: pour the oils, rice vinegar, Chinese 5-spice, ginger, garlic and star anise into a glass or ceramic dish and add the pork. Rub the flavourings into the meat and refrigerate for at least 1 hour.

2 After this time, preheat the grill and grill the pork for 15–20 minutes, turning occasionally.

3 In the meantime, pour the marinade into a large pan and top up with boiling water. Add the noodles and cook for 4–5 minutes, as directed on the packet. Add the pak choi during the last 2 minutes of cooking time. Drain the noodles and pak choi, toss with the sesame oil, and serve with the grilled pork.

110

$\mathcal{V}$ = suitable for vegetarians   ✗ = gluten free   ✗ = dairy free   = source of fibre

Roast pork with Asian slaw

If you have kids who refuse to eat vegetables, this slaw might tempt them! It's colourful, crunchy and the Asian flavours make a refreshing change from fat-laden coleslaw for adults and children alike.

PREPARATION TIME: less than 30 minutes + marinating time

COOKING TIME: 3 hours

SERVES 4–6

For the pork:

4 cloves of garlic,
   peeled and crushed
4-cm (1½-in) piece of ginger,
   peeled and grated
1 Tbsp soy sauce
1 shoulder of pork,
   around 2 kg (4 lb 6 oz) in weight
20 whole cloves

For the slaw:

4 Chinese leaves, shredded
½ head small white cabbage, shredded
2 pak choi, shredded
2 carrots, grated
Bunch of radishes, thinly sliced
200 g (7 oz) tinned water chestnuts,
   drained and rinsed, thinly sliced
Good pinch of ground ginger
1 tsp sesame seeds
½ tsp sesame oil
1 tsp vegetable oil
1 tsp rice vinegar
1 Tbsp of cashew nuts, roughly chopped

111

1 Start by preparing the pork: mix together the garlic, ginger, soy sauce and 1 tablespoon of water. Open up the pork and stud with the cloves, then rub in the garlic mix. Roll the pork up again and secure with string. Refrigerate for 3–4 hours.

2 Preheat the oven to 220° C (425° F/gas mark 7). Place the pork on a roasting rack over a tin and place in the oven. Roast for 30 minutes, then turn the oven down to 180° C (350° F/gas mark 4). Cook for 30 minutes per 500 g (1 lb 2 oz), plus 30 minutes in total.

3 During this time, prepare the slaw: mix all the vegetables together with the ginger in a large bowl. Dress with the oils and rice vinegar just before serving and top with the cashew nuts. When the pork is cooked through, leave to cool slightly, then serve with the slaw.

♥ = heart healthy   = counts towards 5-a-day   X = lower fat

Braised pork chops with leeks, white wine and sage

Braising is a moist method of cooking. Meat is browned first and then cooked slowly with liquid, in this case, white wine. This method is ideal for tougher and inexpensive cuts of meat as the moisture and gentle heat soften and relax meat fibres.

PREPARATION TIME: less than 10 minutes

COOKING TIME: 30 minutes

SERVES 2

2 pork chops
1 tsp vegetable oil
1 leek, sliced
100 ml (3½ fl oz) white wine
1 tsp dried sage
1 Tbsp reduced fat crème fraîche
Freshly ground black pepper

1 Preheat a non-stick frying pan. Brush the pork chops lightly with the oil and place in the centre of the pan. Over a medium-high heat, brown the pork on both sides, then transfer to a plate.

2 Add the leek to the pan and cook for 2 minutes. Pour over the wine and deglaze the pan, that is, use a wooden spoon to scrape up any brown bits from the pan. Add the sage and return the pork to the pan. Cook, half covered, for 15–20 minutes, until the pork is no longer pink in the middle. Transfer the pork to a plate and cover with foil to keep warm. Stir the crème fraîche into the leeks and season with freshly ground black pepper.

112

$\mathcal{V}$ = suitable for vegetarians   ✕ = gluten free   ✕ = dairy free   ⁑ = source of fibre

Braised pork chops with apples

The best known use for juniper berries is as an aromatic flavouring in gin! But these dark, shiny berries work beautifully with pork. You should be able to find juniper berries in the herbs and spices aisle in the supermarket, or in health food stores.

PREPARATION TIME: less than 10 minutes
COOKING TIME: less than 30 minutes
SERVES 2

2 pork chops
½ tsp vegetable oil
3 allspice berries, cracked open
3 juniper berries, cracked open
2 small or 1 large cooking apples, peeled and cut into bite-sized chunks
100 ml (3½ fl oz) cider
½ tsp runny honey
Freshly ground black pepper

113

1 Preheat a non-stick frying pan. Brush the pork chops lightly with the oil and place in the centre of the pan. Over a medium-high heat, brown the pork on both sides, then transfer to a plate.

2 Crack the allspice and juniper berries open using a pestle and mortar or the end of a rolling pin and a bowl. Add these to the pan, cook over a low heat for a couple of minutes, then add the apple pieces. Cook for 3 minutes, then stir in the cider and honey and return the pork to the pan. Cook, half covered for 15–20 minutes, until the pork is no longer pink in the middle. Season with freshly ground black pepper before serving.

♥ = heart healthy   🍎 = counts towards 5-a-day   ✗ = lower fat

Italian-style meatballs with tomato sauce

Although pork and beef are used in this recipe, it's fine to mix and match – turkey, pork, beef and minced lamb will all work here. White meat and poultry will lower the fat content of the meatballs, while red meat adds depth of flavour and moisture. Meatballs can be oven-baked but cooking them in the tomato sauce helps keep them moist and delicious!

PREPARATION TIME: less than 20 minutes
COOKING TIME: 1 hour or more
SERVES 4–6

For the tomato sauce:
1 tsp olive oil
1 onion, peeled and chopped
1 stalk of celery, diced
1 small carrot, diced
2 cloves of garlic, peeled and crushed
2 rashers of bacon, roughly chopped
400 g (14 oz) tinned chopped tomatoes
½ Tbsp tomato purée

For the meatballs:
230 g (8 oz) minced pork
230 g (8 oz) lean minced beef
1 small onion, peeled
2 cloves of garlic, peeled
1 egg
2 Tbsp wholegrain breadcrumbs
2 Tbsp grated Parmesan cheese
1 tsp dried mixed herbs

Tagliatelle, to serve

1 Start by making the tomato sauce: in a large saucepan, heat the olive oil and add the onion, diced celery and carrot. Cook over a medium-high heat for 2 minutes, then reduce the heat, cover and allow to sweat for 8 minutes, stirring occasionally. Add the garlic and bacon, and cook for a further 3 minutes. Pour in the tomatoes and tomato purée, and cover and simmer for 30 minutes. After this time, liquidize using either the blender attachment of the food processor or a hand-held immersion blender.

2 To prepare the meatballs, combine all the ingredients for the meatballs in a large bowl and mix well. Take dessertspoonfuls of the mix and roll into balls. Place the meatballs, in a single layer, into the saucepan with the tomato sauce and cook, covered, for 15–20 minutes, depending on the size of your meatballs. Serve with tagliatelle.

$\mathcal{V}$ = suitable for vegetarians   ✕ = gluten free   ✕ = dairy free   ≈ source of fibre

Lamb-stuffed peppers

This is an unusual way to reach your five portions of fruit and vegetables per day. Many people find peppers too strong or find that they cause heartburn, but cooking the peppers in the oven brings out their sweetness. This works well with the richness of the Moroccan-inspired flavours in the lamb.

PREPARATION TIME: less than 10 minutes

COOKING TIME: 1 hour

SERVES 4

450 g (1 lb) minced lamb
1 onion, peeled and finely sliced
2 cloves of garlic, peeled and crushed
½ tsp cinnamon
½ tsp ground cumin
1 Tbsp tomato purée
2 Tbsp pine nuts
4 red peppers

115

1 Preheat the oven to 180° C (350° F/gas mark 4). Turn the heat on under a medium-sized pan and add the minced lamb – bringing up the temperature will allow excess fat to be drained off, without the meat sticking. Cook for around 8 minutes to brown, then drain off excess fat by tipping the meat into a sieve or colander. Return the meat to the pan and add the onion and garlic. Cook for 4 minutes to soften the onion slightly, then add the cinnamon, cumin and tomato purée. Cook, uncovered, for 15 minutes.

2 In the meantime, heat a small frying pan and dry-fry the pine nuts for around 8 minutes until toasted and aromatic. Keep watching these as they burn easily. Then stir into the minced lamb.

3 Cut the tops off the peppers, about 2 cm (¾ in) from the stalk. Scoop out the seeds and white membranes. Arrange the peppers in a soufflé dish or similar dish that will keep them upright. Fill the peppers with the lamb and place high in the oven for 30 minutes.

♥ = heart healthy   = counts towards 5-a-day   = lower fat

poultry

Southern baked chicken

When you make the decision to eat more healthily, some things are generally off the menu, including southern fried chicken. This version is every bit as tasty but is low in fat since it's cooked in the oven, not the deep fat fryer!

PREPARATION TIME: less than 10 minutes
COOKING TIME: 30–60 minutes
SERVES 2

For the seasoning:
2 Tbsp wholegrain flour
¼ tsp cayenne pepper
1 tsp paprika
1 tsp oregano
½ tsp thyme
½ tsp mustard powder
¼ tsp celery salt
Salt and freshly ground black pepper

For the chicken:
4 chicken portions, such as thighs
   or drumsticks
4 Tbsp semi-skimmed milk

1 Preheat the oven to 220° C (425° F/gas mark 7). Combine all the ingredients for the seasoning and place in a plastic freezer bag.

2 To prepare the chicken, remove the skin from the chicken portions, brush with the milk and then place in the bag with the seasoning mix. Give the bag a good shake, so the chicken becomes coated in seasoning.

3 Place the chicken portions on a baking tray and bake, high in the oven, for 10 minutes. Reduce the heat to 180° C (350° F/gas mark 4) and bake for a further 30–40 minutes, until no longer pink.

118

𝒱 = suitable for vegetarians   ✗ = gluten free   ✗ = dairy free   = source of fibre

Pasta with tarragon chicken and fennel

Tarragon and fennel both have aniseedy flavours so they work well together in this simple dish. If you prefer, use chicken pieces and toss the chicken and strips of cooked fennel into the pasta with a teaspoon of reduced fat crème fraîche.

PREPARATION TIME: less than 10 minutes + marinating time

COOKING TIME: less than 30 minutes

SERVES 2

1 Tbsp extra virgin olive oil
1 Tbsp red wine vinegar
Small bunch of tarragon
2 chicken fillets
100 g (3½ oz) pasta
1 small bulb of fennel
1 tsp olive oil

119

1 Combine the extra virgin olive oil, red wine vinegar and half the tarragon leaves in a glass or ceramic dish and add the chicken fillets. Refrigerate for 1 hour.

2 After this time, preheat a griddle pan. Place the chicken fillets in the centre of the pan and cook, keeping the heat quite high, for 10–12 minutes, until the chicken is cooked through and no longer pink in the middle.

3 In the meantime, bring a large saucepan of water to the boil and boil the pasta for 8–12 minutes, following package directions. When the chicken is cooked, set aside and keep warm.

4 Cut the fennel bulb into slices 1–2 cm (½ in) thick. Brush lightly with the olive oil and cook on the griddle pan for 6–8 minutes, until softened.

5 Drain the pasta and tear in the rest of the tarragon leaves. Serve the pasta topped with the chicken fillet, cut into thick slices, and the griddled fennel.

♥ = heart healthy   🍎 = counts towards 5-a-day   ✗ = lower fat

Chicken pockets with sun-dried tomatoes, red pesto and mozzarella

For this recipe, you need to butterfly the chicken fillets. This is easier than it sounds, especially if you have a very sharp filleting knife. If you prefer, it's fine to place the chicken between two pieces of cling-film and pound them flat with a meat mallet, rolling pin or empty bottle.

PREPARATION TIME: less than 20 minutes
COOKING TIME: less than 30 minutes
SERVES 2

2 balls of frozen spinach
2 chicken fillets
2 tsp red pesto
6 sun-dried tomatoes in oil, drained
½ ball of buffalo mozzarella, sliced

120

1 Preheat the oven to 200° C (400° F/gas mark 6). Set the spinach aside to thaw or defrost in the microwave. Drain out excess water by pressing with a fork.

2 To butterfly the chicken fillets, set the fillets on a chopping board and, using a very sharp knife, cut the fillets on the horizontal, so they open out like a book. Spread the cut surfaces of the fillets with red pesto and then cover one half with the tomatoes, thawed spinach and mozzarella. Place on a baking tray and bake for 15–20 minutes, until the chicken is no longer pink.

$\mathcal{V}$ = suitable for vegetarians   ✗ = gluten free   ✗ = dairy free   = source of fibre

Turkey with Parma ham

**Traditional saltimbocca uses veal but turkey is just as nice – and is
more readily available. Thin pork escalopes can also be used,
as can chicken fillets. Serve with plenty of green vegetables
and pasta or boiled new potatoes.**

PREPARATION TIME: less than 10 minutes
COOKING TIME: less than 10 minutes
SERVES 2

2 turkey steaks, about 150 g (5½ oz) each
2 slices of Parma ham
2 sage leaves
1 tsp olive oil
10 g (⅓ oz) butter
75 ml (2½ fl oz) Marsala

121

1 Place the turkey steaks between two pieces of cling-film and pound them flat
with a meat mallet, rolling pin or empty bottle. They need to be 1–2 cm (½ in) in
thickness.

2 Lay a slice of Parma ham over the turkey, top that with a sage leaf and secure
them together with a cocktail stick.

3 Heat the oil and butter together in a non-stick pan and add the turkey. Keeping
the heat high, cook for 3 minutes, turn and pour in the Marsala. Bring this to the
boil, then simmer for about 3 minutes and serve.

Turkey with soy, honey and mustard

This turkey could be baked, cooked on the griddle pan or grilled but grilling is quick and easy and it's a method that works just as well for the pepper strips and the turkey.

PREPARATION TIME: less than 10 minutes + marinating time
COOKING TIME: less than 30 minutes
SERVES 2

1 Tbsp rich soy sauce
1 tsp runny honey
1 tsp mustard
1 Tbsp water
2 turkey steaks, around 180 g (6½ oz) each
1 red pepper, cut into thick strips
1 yellow pepper, cut into thick strips
1 tsp vegetable oil

1 Combine the soy sauce, honey, mustard and water in a glass or ceramic dish and use to coat the turkey steaks. Refrigerate for about 1 hour.

2 Cook under a preheated grill for 20–25 minutes, depending on the thickness of the turkey, until the turkey is no longer pink in the middle.

3 While the turkey is cooking, brush the peppers lightly with oil. Grill alongside the turkey for the last 10–15 minutes of cooking time, turning occasionally.

$\mathcal{V}$ = suitable for vegetarians   ✗ = gluten free   ✗ = dairy free   = source of fibre

Lime, coconut and sesame kebabs

These kebabs are ideal for the barbecue! Serve with a dipping sauce of sweet chilli sauce, soy sauce and ginger, and warmed wholemeal pitta breads.

PREPARATION TIME: less than 10 minutes + marinating time

COOKING TIME: less than 30 minutes

SERVES 2

1 Tbsp creamed coconut
Juice of 1 lime
1 tsp sesame oil
250 g (9 oz) turkey pieces
1 tsp sesame seeds

1 Place the creamed coconut in a bowl and add the lime juice. Stir to dissolve and add the sesame oil. Use this mix to coat the turkey pieces and set aside for 30 minutes in the refrigerator.

2 Thread the turkey pieces onto skewers and cook on a preheated griddle pan for 15–20 minutes, turning occasionally. Sprinkle with sesame seeds before serving.

♥ = heart healthy   🍎 = counts towards 5-a-day   ✗ = lower fat

Chicken sandwich with pesto, mozzarella and rocket

Chicken fillets cooked with the bone in and skin left on can be more moist than skinned and boned versions. Baking them on a rack allows excess fat to drip away and as long as the skin is removed before eating, these aren't too different in terms of fat and calories from griddled skinless fillets.

PREPARATION TIME: less than 10 minutes
COOKING TIME: 30–60 minutes
SERVES 2

2 small chicken fillets, bone-in, skin on
2 multi-grain demi-baguettes
2 tsp of your favourite pesto
½ ball of buffalo mozzarella, sliced
Bag of rocket or other strongly flavoured salad leaves

1 Preheat the oven to 200° C (400° F/gas mark 6). Place the chicken on the rack of a grill pan, over a baking tray, and roast in the oven for 30–35 minutes.

2 Place the baguettes in the oven during the last 5 minutes of cooking time to warm through, or according to package directions if using part-baked rolls.

3 Remove the skin from the cooked chicken and pull off the meat – this is easiest using two forks. Split the baguettes open and spread each with 1 teaspoon of pesto. Add the chicken and top with a couple of slices of mozzarella. Return to the oven for 3 minutes to melt the mozzarella. Top with a handful of rocket before serving.

124

V = suitable for vegetarians   X = gluten free   X = dairy free   = source of fibre

Chicken fajitas

Chocolate might seem like a strange addition to chilli but, even though only a little is used, it gives a touch of sweetness and richness. Tomatoes often need something to counteract their acidity so chocolate is just the thing in this case!

PREPARATION TIME: less than 20 minutes
COOKING TIME: less than 30 minutes
SERVES 3

2 tsp olive oil
200 g (7 oz) chicken pieces
1 onion, peeled and sliced
1 small red pepper, cut into strips
1 small yellow pepper, cut into strips
2 cloves of garlic, peeled and crushed
2 red chillis, finely chopped
½ tsp ground cumin
½ tsp chilli powder
½ oregano
400 g (14 oz) tinned chopped tomatoes
2 tsp tomato purée
Juice of ½ lime
1 square of dark chocolate
Flour tortillas and salad, to serve

1 Heat 1 teaspoon of oil in a non-stick frying pan and add the chicken pieces. Over a medium-high heat, seal these on all sides and remove to a plate.

2 Add the remaining oil to the pan and cook the onion, peppers, garlic and chilli for 8–10 minutes to soften. Stir in the cumin, chilli powder and oregano and cook for a couple of minutes. Pour in the chopped tomatoes, tomato purée and lime juice and return the chicken to the pan. Bring to the boil and simmer, half covered, for 20 minutes. After this time, add the chocolate, stir to melt and serve with flour tortillas and salad.

125

♥ = heart healthy   🍎 = counts towards 5-a-day   ✗ = lower fat

Chicken with pesto yoghurt marinade

These pitta pockets carry through the flavours from the pesto, using basil as part of the salad and topping with toasted pine nuts. It would be fine to add shavings of Parmesan over the top of the chicken, too, when serving. When marinating chicken in dairy-based products like milk, yoghurt or buttermilk, be sure to leave them for no more than 30 minutes, otherwise the chicken can become 'woolly' in texture.

PREPARATION TIME: less than 10 minutes + marinating time
COOKING TIME: less than 20 minutes
SERVES 2

For the chicken:
2 Tbsp low-fat natural yoghurt
1 heaped tsp pesto
2 chicken fillets

2 tsp pine nuts
2 wholegrain pitta breads
Mixed salad leaves
Small bunch of basil
2 tsp extra virgin olive oil
Good squeeze of lemon juice

1 Start by preparing the chicken. Place the yoghurt in a glass or ceramic dish and stir in the pesto. Use to coat the chicken fillets and refrigerate for 30 minutes.

2 Preheat a griddle pan and place the chicken fillets in the centre of the pan. Cook over a high heat for 5 minutes without moving, then turn over and cook for a further 8–10 minutes, until cooked through and no longer pink in the middle.

3 In the meantime, heat a small pan and dry-fry the pine nuts for around 6 minutes, until golden and aromatic. Toast the pitta pockets, slice open and half-fill with a mix of salad leaves and basil. Add thick slices of chicken and top with the toasted pine nuts. Drizzle with olive oil and lemon juice before serving.

$\mathcal{V}$ = suitable for vegetarians χ = gluten free χ = dairy free   = source of fibre

Thai chicken skewers

These skewers are extremely quick and easy to make – just remember to soak wooden or bamboo skewers in water for at least 20 minutes before cooking to prevent them burning under the grill. Serve these skewers with a mix of boiled basmati and wild rice, and a little sweet chilli sauce for dipping.

PREPARATION TIME: less than 10 minutes + marinating time
COOKING TIME: less than 30 minutes
SERVES 2

1 Tbsp creamed coconut
1 Tbsp Thai green curry paste
250 g (9 oz) chicken pieces
Juice of ½ lime

1 Place the creamed coconut into a heat-proof bowl and add 2 tablespoons boiling water. Set aside to dissolve and cool. Stir in the curry paste and use to coat the chicken pieces. Refrigerate for 30 minutes.

2 After this time, thread the chicken pieces onto skewers and cook under a preheated grill for 15 minutes, turning occasionally. Squeeze over the juice of the lime before serving.

127

fish

Tuna steak with Greek salad

Many of us will be familiar with the kind of tuna that comes in tins but while this is extremely convenient and a relatively cheap source of protein, the canning process destroys the essential fatty acids that make oily fish so healthy. Fresh tuna, however, is a great source of unsaturated fats so choose this when you can. It only takes a few minutes to cook, since longer cooking can give it a rubbery or chewy texture. Don't be afraid to eat it rare!

PREPARATION TIME: less than 10 minutes
COOKING TIME: less than 10 minutes
SERVES 2

For the salad:
1 small gem lettuce
2 ripe plum tomatoes, quartered
75 g (2½ oz) feta cheese
16 black or green olives (or a mix of both)
1 Tbsp extra virgin olive oil
½ lemon

For the fish:
2 tuna steaks, around 200 g (7 oz) each
1 tsp light olive oil

1 Start by preparing the salad. Place the washed lettuce in a large bowl and toss in the tomatoes. Crumble over the feta cheese and sprinkle over the olives.

2 For the fish, brush the tuna lightly with olive oil and place in the centre of a preheated griddle pan. Cook over a high heat for 3–4 minutes on each side – the tuna should still be red in the centre. Drizzle the olive oil and lemon juice over the salad and serve with the tuna steaks.

$\mathcal{V}$ = suitable for vegetarians   ✗ = gluten free   ✗ = dairy free   = source of fibre

Cajun salmon

Since this seasoning blend uses so many different herbs and spices, you might want to double or triple the amounts and keep it in a jam jar or other air-tight container. It is best to store spices in the dark – a dark drawer, for example – as light can impair their colour and flavour.

PREPARATION TIME: less than 10 minutes
COOKING TIME: less than 30 minutes
SERVES 2

For the Cajun seasoning:
½ tsp of each: salt and freshly ground black pepper
¼ tsp of each: garlic powder, ground coriander, cumin, ground fennel seed, dried thyme and oregano

For the fish:
2 salmon fillets, around 200 g (7 oz) each
1 tsp mustard, mixed with 1 tsp water

1 Preheat the oven to 200° C (400° F/gas mark 6). Combine all the seasoning ingredients in a small bowl.

2 Place the salmon fillets on a non-stick baking tray and lightly brush the top of the fillets with the diluted mustard. Sprinkle around 1 teaspoon of seasoning over each fillet and press this down with the back of a spoon or your fingers. Bake high in the oven for 10 minutes.

131

= heart healthy   = counts towards 5-a-day   = lower fat

Pasta with smoked fish and peas

This dish is extremely quick and easy to make. There is barely any preparation involved as the fish is cooked and the sauce prepared whilst the pasta is boiling. The mild creamy sauce complements the stronger flavour of the fish beautifully.

PREPARATION TIME: less than 10 minutes
COOKING TIME: less than 30 minutes
SERVES 2

100 g (3½ oz) pasta
100 ml (3½ fl oz) semi-skimmed milk
100 ml (3½ fl oz) white wine
Good pinch of saffron
2 fillets of smoked haddock
100 g (3½ oz) peas
Good squeeze of lemon juice
1 level Tbsp reduced fat crème fraîche
1 Tbsp chopped fresh parsley

1 Bring a large pan of water to the boil and boil the pasta for 8–12 minutes, following package directions.

2 Pour the milk and white wine into a wide pan and add the saffron. Bring to the boil, add the fish fillets and reduce the heat. Poach the fish for 5 minutes, then transfer to a plate and flake the fish, discarding any bones.

3 Bring the milk and wine mix back to a fast boil and allow to boil until the volume is reduced to 4 tablespoons. Add the peas and bring back to a boil for a further 2–3 minutes. Squeeze in the lemon juice and stir in the crème fraîche and parsley.

4 Drain the pasta and stir this into the sauce. Top with the flaked fish before serving.

132

$\mathcal{V}$ = suitable for vegetarians   ✗ = gluten free   ✗ = dairy free   = source of fibre

Red mullet with lemon and garlic

Fish is an integral part of the Mediterranean diet. Oily fish, rich in unsaturated fats, helps lower unhealthy LDL cholesterol while boosting levels of healthy HDL cholesterol. White fish is a low fat, low calorie way to obtain high quality protein in the diet. We should all aim to eat fish three to four times per week.

PREPARATION TIME: less than 10 minutes + marinating time
COOKING TIME: less than 20 minutes
SERVES 2

1 lemon
2 red mullet, scaled
Small bunch of flat leaf parsley
2 cloves of garlic, peeled and sliced
1 tsp olive oil

133

1 Preheat the oven to 200° C (400° F/gas mark 6). Using a potato peeler, cut 4 large strips of peel from the lemon. Place this inside the cavity of the fish, along with the parsley, stalks and all, and the garlic. Set aside for 30 minutes to allow the flavours to infuse.

2 Brush the fish lightly with the oil and place on a baking tray. Place in the preheated oven and bake for 8–10 minutes. Squeeze over a little lemon juice when serving.

♥ = heart healthy   = counts towards 5-a-day   ✗ = lower fat

Sea bass with Asian spices

Bass is a very lean fish and is very versatile, being suitable for grilling, griddling, baking or, as in this recipe, steaming. Bass has a mild flavour, so here we are steaming the fish over a pan of water infused with the aromatic flavours of lemongrass, chilli and ginger.

PREPARATION TIME: 10 minutes
COOKING TIME: less than 20 minutes
SERVES 2

2 stalks of lemongrass
1 red chilli
4-cm (1½-in) piece of ginger
2 sea bass
Small bunch of coriander

134

1 Remove the tough outer stalks from the lemongrass and set aside. Top and tail the chilli and remove the seeds and any white pith. Peel the ginger. Place the trimmings from all of these aromatics into a large steamer saucepan and pour over boiling water to a depth of approximately 5 cm (2 in).

2 Pound the more tender, inner lemongrass stalks with the handle of your knife to release their aromatic oils. Slice the chilli and ginger quite thickly and place these flavourings into the cavity of the fish, then place the fish in the steamer basket.

3 Set the steamer basket in place over the boiling, scented water and steam the fish for 8–10 minutes, until it flakes easily. Remove the flavourings before eating.

$\mathcal{V}$ = suitable for vegetarians   ✗ = gluten free   ✗ = dairy free   ≈ = source of fibre

Fish curry

Tamarind paste is made from the pods of the tamarind tree. It imparts a tart, sweet and sour flavour and is available as a paste, juice or pressed pulp. Use more or less to your own taste.

PREPARATION TIME: less than 10 minutes
COOKING TIME: less than 30 minutes
SERVES 4

For the fish:
450 g (1 lb) white fish, such as cod or hoki
½ tsp ground coriander
½ tsp cumin
½ tsp turmeric
½ tsp chilli powder

For the sauce:
1 tsp tamarind paste
1 tsp creamed coconut
1 tsp vegetable oil
1 onion, peeled and thinly sliced
2 cloves or garlic, peeled and crushed
4-cm (1½-in) piece of ginger, peeled and grated
2 tomatoes, diced

Boiled basmati rice, to serve

1 Start by preparing the fish. Cut the fish into 3–4 cm (1½-in) pieces. Mix the spices together and use to lightly coat the fish pieces. Set aside.

2 To make the sauce, place the tamarind paste and creamed coconut in a small bowl, pour over 100 ml (3½ fl oz) boiling water and allow to dissolve. Heat the oil in a non-stick frying pan and add the onion, garlic and ginger. Cook over a medium-low heat for 8 minutes to soften. Add the tomatoes, dissolved tamarind and coconut and bring to the boil. Reduce the heat, then simmer for 10 minutes. Add the pieces of fish and simmer for a further 10 minutes. Serve with boiled basmati rice.

135

♥ = heart healthy   🍎 = counts towards 5-a-day   ✗ = lower fat

Salmon and leek parcels

Cooking in parcels is a no-fuss, no-hassle way to prepare fish.
Simply make a parcel from aluminium foil and add any flavourings
of your choice – go for Oriental flavours with ginger, soy sauce and
sesame, or follow Mediterranean traditions with plenty of fresh herbs
and garlic, or use this recipe for a more classic combination of salmon
with leeks and white wine.

PREPARATION TIME: less than 10 minutes
COOKING TIME: less than 20 minutes
SERVES 2

1 small leek, thinly sliced
4 sprigs of fresh thyme
2 salmon fillets, around 200 g (7 oz) each
2 Tbsp white wine
Freshly ground black pepper
20 g (¾ oz) butter

Preheat the oven to 200° C (400° F/gas mark 6). Cut two 20-cm (8-in) squares
of aluminium foil. Divide the sliced leek between the pieces of foil, add the
sprigs of thyme and place the salmon fillets on top. Spoon over the white
wine, season with freshly ground black pepper and top with a knob of butter.
Seal the parcels, place them on a baking tray and place high in the preheated
oven for 12–15 minutes, until the salmon is opaque and flakes easily.

136

$\mathcal{V}$ = suitable for vegetarians   ✗ = gluten free   ✗ = dairy free   = source of fibre

Parma-wrapped monkfish

Monkfish tail is a very firm white fish that retains its texture on cooking. It can be cooked very much like meat so roasting is ideal for this fish. This dish could be served with roast new potatoes or roast mixed vegetables.

PREPARATION TIME: less than 10 minutes
COOKING TIME: less than 30 minutes
SERVES 2

2–4 slices of Parma ham, depending on the size of the fish pieces
2 pieces of monkfish, around 200 g (7 oz) each
4 fresh sage leaves
1–2 tsp olive oil

Preheat the oven to 190° C (375° F/gas mark 5). Lay 1 or 2 slices of Parma ham (depending on how many you are using) on a plate, place a piece of monkfish over it and top with two sage leaves. Wrap the Parma ham around the fish, brush lightly with the oil and place on a baking tray. Repeat with the other fish parcel. Bake in the preheated oven for 25–30 minutes.

137

= heart healthy   = counts towards 5-a-day   = lower fat

Fish cakes

Fish cakes, like fish fingers, are a great way to get kids to eat fish. Serve them with salad and tomato salsa or with lemon butter or tartare sauce for the grown-ups.

PREPARATION TIME: less than 20 minutes

COOKING TIME: 30–60 minutes

SERVES 3–4

450 g (1 lb) white fish, such as cod, haddock or hoki
4 slices of granary bread, made into breadcrumbs
4 spring onions, sliced
2 eggs
2 Tbsp reduced fat mayonnaise
1 level tsp mustard
1 Tbsp chopped fresh parsley
4 small pickled gherkins, diced
2 tsp olive oil

1 Cook the fish by poaching it for 10 minutes or by cooking for 5–6 minutes in the microwave. Flake the fish and transfer it to a large bowl. Add the remaining ingredients and mix well, adding 1–2 tablespoons of water if necessary. Take a handful of the mix and shape it into a patty. Repeat until the mixture is finished. You should be able to make three or four patties with these quantities. Set on a plate and refrigerate for 20–30 minutes.

2 Preheat the oven to 180° C (350° F/gas mark 4). Place the fish cakes on a baking tray and brush lightly with the oil. Turn over, brush the other side with oil and bake for 15–20 minutes, turning once during the cooking time.

138

$\mathcal{V}$ = suitable for vegetarians   ✗ = gluten free   ✗ = dairy free   = source of fibre

Salmon with rice noodles

This recipe uses flat-leaf parsley almost like a salad leaf. Both flat-leaf and curly parsley are packed with nutrients, especially vitamin C, vitamin A, folate and iron. They also contain oils that are powerful anti-carcinogens. Parsley is so much more than a garnish!

PREPARATION TIME: less than 10 minutes
COOKING TIME: less than 10 minutes
SERVES 2

2 fillets of salmon, around 200 g (7 oz) each
2 bundles of rice noodles
2 Tbsp flaked almonds
2 mild red chillis, sliced
Bunch of flat-leaf parsley
Juice of ½ a lime
2 tsp extra virgin olive oil

139

1 Steam the salmon fillets for 5–6 minutes or cook them in the microwave for 2–3 minutes.

2 In the meantime, prepare the rice noodles: place them in a large bowl and pour over boiling water to cover. Set aside for 4 minutes, or as directed on the pack.

3 Heat a small pan and add the almonds. Toast them until golden and aromatic, for about 6 minutes. Keep watching and stirring these as they burn easily.

4 Flake the cooked salmon into large pieces and toss with the drained rice noodles. Add the sliced red chillis and plenty of torn flat-leaf parsley and top with the toasted flaked almonds. Drizzle with the lime juice and olive oil just before serving.

 = heart healthy   = counts towards 5-a-day   = lower fat

Smoked mackerel and cucumber salad

Mackerel is an oily fish and has more omega-3 fatty acids than any other fish going! Serve this dish as a light lunch, or make it more substantial by adding rice noodles or boiled basmati rice.

PREPARATION TIME: less than 10 minutes + marinating time

COOKING TIME: none

SERVES 2

½ cucumber
½ Tbsp light soy sauce
½ Tbsp sherry
½ Tbsp rice vinegar
1 tsp sugar
1 red chilli, sliced
2 fillets of ready-to-eat smoked mackerel

1 Cut the cucumber in half lengthways and in half again. Cut out the seeds in the centre and slice the cucumber into sticks about 6 cm (2½ in) long.

2 Combine the soy sauce, sherry, rice vinegar, sugar and chilli in a glass or ceramic bowl and add the cucumber. Set aside for 15 minutes for the flavours to infuse. Serve on the side with the smoked mackerel.

$\mathcal{V}$ = suitable for vegetarians   ✗ = gluten free   = dairy free   = source of fibre

Potato salad with trout

Most commercially prepared potato salads are full of sugar as well as being loaded with fat. This version uses a mix of yoghurt and crème fraîche, with plenty of herbs to lower the fat content while still providing plenty of flavour.

PREPARATION TIME: less than 10 minutes
COOKING TIME: 30–60 minutes
SERVES 2

For the potato salad:
200 g (7 oz) small new potatoes
1 Tbsp low-fat natural yoghurt
1 Tbsp reduced fat crème fraîche
2 tsp capers, roughly chopped
1 Tbsp chopped fresh dill
Salt and freshly ground black pepper

141

For the fish:
2 whole trout
Bunch of parsley, chopped
4 sprigs of thyme, chopped
1 tsp fennel seeds

1 Boil the potatoes for 15–18 minutes until tender. Drain and set aside to cool for 10 minutes, then stir in the remaining ingredients for the potato salad.

2 Preheat the oven to 180° C (350° F/gas mark 4). Fill the cavity of the fish with the herbs and fennel seeds. Place on a baking tray and bake for 20 minutes, then serve with the potato salad.

= heart healthy   = counts towards 5-a-day   = lower fat

sides and snacks

Sweetcorn relish

You'll never eat jarred relish again once you try this home-made version! This is additive-free, packed with fibre and vitamin A and isn't sickly sweet. Serve it on top of burgers, with Fish cakes (p 138) or with Southern baked chicken (p 118).

PREPARATION TIME: less than 10 minutes
COOKING TIME: less than 30 minutes
SERVES 4–6

1 red pepper
2 cloves of garlic, unpeeled
1 Tbsp extra virgin olive oil
2 cobs of sweetcorn or 400 g (14 oz) tinned sweetcorn,
    no added sugar or salt
2 tsp of red wine vinegar
1 tsp of balsamic vinegar
½ tsp honey
Good pinch of chilli powder

1 Preheat the oven to 200° C (400° F/gas mark 6). Cut the red pepper into quarters and remove the seeds and pith. Place on a baking tray, along with the garlic and drizzle with olive oil. Roast for around 25 minutes or until softened and beginning to blacken at the edges.

2 In the meantime, boil the sweetcorn for 6 minutes. Drain and when cool enough to handle, cut the corn kernels off the cob. Combine the corn, diced roast pepper, roast garlic squeezed from its papery skin, vinegars, honey and chilli powder in a saucepan and bring to a simmer. Simmer for 5–10 minutes before serving with grilled chicken, fish cakes or burgers.

$\mathcal{V}$ = suitable for vegetarians   X = gluten free   X = dairy free   = source of fibre

Bombay potatoes

These potatoes can be cooked in the oven just as easily as on the hob. In a baking tray, heat the oil and spices together for 10 minutes at 190° C (375° F/gas mark 5) while the potatoes par boil, then toss in the drained potatoes.

PREPARATION TIME: less than 10 minutes
COOKING TIME: less than 30 minutes
SERVES 4

500 g (1 lb 2 oz) mini new potatoes
1 Tbsp vegetable oil
1 tsp mustard seeds
1 tsp coriander seeds
1 tsp cumin seeds
½ tsp garam masala
2 Tbsp low-fat natural yoghurt

145

1 Par boil the new potatoes for 10–15 minutes, until almost tender. Drain and set aside.

2 Heat the oil in a non-stick frying pan. Add the mustard, coriander and cumin seeds and cook over a medium-high heat until they are aromatic and start to pop. Keeping the heat high, add the potatoes and cook, stirring all the time, for 8 minutes. The potatoes should start to crisp on the outside and become golden. Sprinkle over the garam masala, cook for a further 2 minutes and serve with a dollop of yoghurt on the side.

♥ = heart healthy   = counts towards 5-a-day   ✗ = lower fat

Celeriac remoulade

The root vegetable celeriac isn't quite so popular as carrots, parsnips, swedes and turnips, but it is now becoming widely available and more people are enjoying its strong celery flavour, raw and cooked.

PREPARATION TIME: less than 20 minutes

COOKING TIME: none

SERVES 4

50 g (2 oz) walnuts

For the remoulade sauce:
1 Tbsp reduced fat mayonnaise
2 Tbsp low-fat natural yoghurt
2 tsp capers, roughly chopped
2 anchovy fillets, very finely chopped
¼ tsp paprika
¼ tsp mustard powder
Dash of Worcestershire sauce
1 Tbsp chopped parsley

For the vegetables:
1 small celeriac
2 small carrots
¼ white cabbage

1 Heat a small frying pan and add the walnuts. Dry-fry for 6–7 minutes, stirring all the time, until toasted and aromatic. Watch these carefully as they will burn easily. Set aside to cool, then roughly chop.

2 In a bowl, combine all the ingredients for the sauce and set aside.

3 Grate the celeriac and carrots (the food processor will make short work of this) and finely shred the cabbage. Transfer to a bowl and stir in the sauce, coating all the vegetables. Top with the walnuts.

𝒱 = suitable for vegetarians   ✗ = gluten free   ✗ = dairy free   ⋯ = source of fibre

Beetroot and sweet potato crisps

Baking crisps instead of deep-frying them keeps the fat content down. Beetroot and sweet potatoes pack in more nutrients than potatoes and you also get to control how much salt to add to your crisps. Leave out the salt completely and try flavouring your vegetable crisps with black pepper, paprika or thyme, or use chilli, lemon or pepper oil.

PREPARATION TIME: less than 20 minutes
COOKING TIME: 30–60 minutes
SERVES 2–4

1 beetroot, around 200 g (7 oz)
1 sweet potato, around 200 g (7 oz)
2 Tbsp olive oil
Sea salt

147

1 Preheat the oven to 200° C (400° F/gas mark 6). Peel the beetroot and sweet potato and then, still using the peeler (or a mandolin or food processor), cut the beetroot and sweet potato into very thin slices, cutting them into separate bowls. Add 1 tablespoon of olive oil to each bowl and toss well so all the vegetable slices are coated lightly in oil.

2 Place the beetroot and sweet potato slices onto separate baking trays, in a single layer if possible, and place high in the oven. The beetroot will take 30–40 minutes, and the sweet potato, 25–30 minutes. Check and toss the vegetable crisps often. When dried out and crisp, place on kitchen paper before sprinkling with sea salt.

❤ = heart healthy   🍎 = counts towards 5-a-day   ✕ = lower fat

Indian-style vegetables

This dish can be served as part of an Indian meal or to accompany a piece of marinated and grilled chicken, but also makes a meal in itself, served with boiled brown or basmati rice or packed into a toasted wholemeal pitta bread.

PREPARATION TIME: less than 20 minutes
COOKING TIME: less than 30 minutes
SERVES 2–3

1 tsp vegetable oil
1 onion, peeled
2 cloves of garlic, peeled and crushed
2-cm (¾-in) piece of ginger, grated
½ tsp turmeric
¼ tsp ground cumin
¼ tsp fenugreek
4 ripe tomatoes, each cut into eight
1 courgette, cut into thin coins
150 g (5½ oz) green beans
150 g (5½ oz) peas
6 small florets of broccoli
6 small florets of cauliflower
Small bunch of fresh coriander, chopped

Heat the oil in a non-stick frying pan. Cut half of the onion into thin slices and finely chop the other half. Add to the oil and cook gently for 5–6 minutes without colouring. Add the garlic and ginger and cook for a further 3 minutes. Stir in the spices, then add the tomatoes. Cook for 2–3 minutes to soften the tomatoes. Add a splash of water and stir in the courgette slices. Cook for 5 minutes before adding the remaining vegetables. Cover and cook for a further 5–6 minutes. Sprinkle with chopped fresh coriander before serving.

$\mathcal{V}$ = suitable for vegetarians $\cancel{X}$ = gluten free $\cancel{\cancel{X}}$ = dairy free   = source of fibre

New potatoes with yoghurt and caper dressing

Most commercially-made potato salads are full of sugar and fat. This version is full of nothing but flavour as yoghurt replaces mayonnaise and capers and herbs provide flavour, not fat!

PREPARATION TIME: less than 10 minutes
COOKING TIME: less than 30 minutes
SERVES 4–6

For the potatoes:
500 g (1 lb 2 oz) mini new potatoes

For the dressing:
2 Tbsp low-fat natural yoghurt
1 Tbsp capers, drained and roughly chopped
2 Tbsp chopped fresh mint
1 Tbsp chopped fresh parsley
Salt and freshly ground black pepper

149

1 Boil the potatoes for 15–20 minutes, or until tender. In the meantime, combine all the ingredients for the dressing in a bowl and set aside (not in the fridge).

2 Drain the potatoes, transfer to a large bowl and allow to cool slightly. Gently stir in the dressing while the potatoes are just warm. Serve at room temperature.

 = heart healthy   = counts towards 5-a-day   = lower fat

Balsamic mushrooms

Try to prepare these mushrooms well in advance of serving – at least 2 hours and up to 6 hours ahead. The longer they are left in the marinade, the softer they will become and the more intense a flavour they will develop.

PREPARATION TIME: less than 10 minutes
COOKING TIME: none
SERVES 4–6

For the dressing:
2 cloves of garlic, peeled and crushed with a little salt
1 Tbsp balsamic vinegar
1 Tbsp extra virgin olive oil
Pinch of sugar
Freshly ground black pepper

For the mushrooms:
500 g (1 lb 2 oz) button mushrooms
2 Tbsp chopped curly parsley

1 Place all the dressing ingredients in a jam jar, seal and shake well together.

2 Trim the mushrooms and wipe clean with kitchen paper. Cut into bite-sized chunks and place in a bowl. Pour over the dressing, toss to mix well and set aside for at least 2 hours. Sprinkle with the chopped parsley just before serving.

150

Baby vegetables en papillote

These vegetable parcels are ideal for dinner parties as they can be prepared in advance. You can serve a selection of vegetables without having the table covered in separate serving dishes and your kitchen won't be totally steamed up from boiling vegetables!

PREPARATION TIME: less than 10 minutes

COOKING TIME: less than 30 minutes

SERVES 4

4 baby leeks
8 baby courgettes or small patty pan squash
8 baby carrots
8 asparagus spears
8 small florets of broccoli
4 sprigs of fresh thyme
4 sprigs of fresh rosemary
Freshly ground black pepper
120 ml (4 fl oz) white wine
25 g (1 oz) butter

151

1 Preheat the oven to 190° C (375° F/gas mark 5). Cut four 20-cm (8-in) squares of aluminium foil.

2 Cut the leeks in half lengthways and do the same with the courgettes or patty pan, if they are large. Split the vegetables equally among the four pieces of foil, piling them up in the centre. Tuck a sprig each of thyme and rosemary into each parcel, season with freshly ground black pepper and then draw the corners of the foil into the centre. Spoon 2 tablespoons of wine into each parcel and place a dab of butter on top of the vegetables. Seal the parcels, place on a baking tray and bake for 10–15 minutes.

♥ = heart healthy   = counts towards 5-a-day   ✗ = lower fat

Roast butternut squash

The orange flesh of butternut squash is packed with beta-carotene, vitamin C, magnesium, manganese, potassium and dietary fibre. While squash has a relatively high GI value, serve this dish with pasta, a casserole, or to accompany roast meat or grilled fish, and the overall GI of the meal will be lowered.

PREPARATION TIME: less than 10 minutes
COOKING TIME: 30–60 minutes
SERVES 4–6

1 butternut squash, about 1 kg (2 lb 4 oz)
1–2 Tbsp extra virgin olive oil
Salt and freshly ground black pepper
2 sprigs of fresh rosemary
2 bay leaves

152

Preheat the oven to 190° C (375° F/gas mark 5). Prepare the butternut squash – the easiest way to do this is to cut the squash in half widthways, separating the round bulb end from the straighter section, then peel with a potato peeler. Cut the bulb in half again and remove the seeds with a spoon. Cut into 2.5-cm (1-in) chunks and place on a baking tray. Toss in the olive oil, season with salt and freshly ground black pepper and tuck in the rosemary and bay leaves. Place high in the oven and roast for 30 minutes until tender.

V = suitable for vegetarians   X = gluten free   X = dairy free   = source of fibre

Mixed green vegetables with crème fraîche

The short cooking time of this dish helps retain all the valuable nutrients in the vegetables, as well as their vibrant colours.

PREPARATION TIME: less than 10 minutes
COOKING TIME: less than 10 minutes
SERVES 2

4 Tbsp white wine
150 g (5½ oz) peas
150 g (5½ oz) green beans
150 g (5½ oz) asparagus
200 g (7 oz) baby spinach leaves, rinsed
1 heaped Tbsp reduced fat crème fraîche
Grating of fresh nutmeg

153

Heat the wine in a saucepan and boil until reduced by half in volume. Add the peas and green beans and simmer, covered, for 2 minutes. Add the asparagus and cook for a further 2 minutes. Add the spinach leaves (leave some water on the spinach after rinsing), cover, and cook for a further 3 minutes, until the spinach has wilted. Remove from the heat, stir in the crème fraîche and grate in a little fresh nutmeg (equivalent to about ¼ teaspoon).

= heart healthy ♥ = counts towards 5-a-day = lower fat

Green beans with tomatoes and egg

This is a lovely summery side dish – the vibrant green of the beans, the red tomato and sunny egg colours will brighten up any plate! Serve with roast chicken or just with some crusty wholegrain bread to soak up the dressing.

PREPARATION TIME: less than 20 minutes

COOKING TIME: less than 30 minutes

SERVES 2

For the dressing:
1 Tbsp red wine vinegar
1½ Tbsp extra virgin olive oil
½ tsp mustard, preferably Dijon
Salt and freshly ground black pepper

For the vegetables:
100 g (3½ oz) runner beans
100 g (3½ oz) fine green beans
1 egg
½ red onion, peeled and
 very finely chopped
1 tomato

1 Start by preparing the dressing. Combine all the dressing ingredients in a jam jar, sealing and shaking well together. Set aside.

2 Trim the runner beans and cut them into 2-cm (¾-in) slices. Trim the green beans and cut them into 4-cm (1½-in) pieces.

3 Boil the egg for 10 minutes. At the same time, place a metal sieve over the pan of boiling water to steam the beans: add the runner beans first, steam for 3 minutes then add the green beans and steam for a further 5 minutes.

4 At the end of the cooking time, run the hard-boiled egg under cold water to prevent a grey ring forming around the yolk. Transfer the beans to a bowl and add the red onion. Pour over the dressing while the beans are still warm.

5 Peel the tomato: to do this, pierce the tomato with a sharp knife and place in a heat-proof bowl. Pour over enough boiling water to cover and leave for 30 seconds. Remove from the hot water and plunge into a bowl of iced water. The skin will start to peel away and can be easily slipped off. Dice the tomato finely, removing the seeds, and stir into the beans. Transfer to a serving bowl and top with the finely chopped hard boiled egg.

$\mathcal{V}$ = suitable for vegetarians   X = gluten free   X = dairy free   = source of fibre

Mexican bean and guacamole layer

You could make your own guacamole by mashing ripe avocado with lime juice, chilli, garlic and coriander but lower fat versions are available in supermarkets which makes this dish quicker and easier to prepare.

PREPARATION TIME: less than 10 minutes
COOKING TIME: less than 30 minutes
SERVES 4

1 tsp olive oil
1 small onion, peeled and finely chopped
1 clove of garlic, peeled and crushed
1 red chilli, sliced
2 tomatoes, diced
100 g (3½ oz) each of pinto beans and kidney beans
  (or use just one variety if that's easier)
1 lime
Bunch of fresh coriander, chopped
150-ml (5-fl oz) tub of reduced fat guacamole
150-ml (5-fl oz) tub of reduced fat sour cream

155

1 Heat the oil in a frying pan and add the onion. Cook for 5–6 minutes to soften without colouring. Add the garlic and sliced chilli – leave some of the seeds in if you prefer a hotter dish. Cook for 2–3 minutes, then add the tomatoes, beans and juice of half the lime. Cook, uncovered, for 5 minutes, then remove from the heat and stir in the coriander. Taste and season with more lime juice if preferred, then mash lightly with a potato masher. Spoon into four ramekins and set aside to cool.

2 Once cool, top each serving with a dessertspoonful of guacamole and top that with a teaspoon of sour cream. Finally, top with a sprinkling of coriander. Serve with spiced pitta chips, toasted wholemeal pitta bread or tortilla chips with extra lime wedges on the side.

♥ = heart healthy   🍎 = counts towards 5-a-day   ✕ = lower fat

Rice with black-eye bean salsa

Piri piri is a Portuguese hot pepper sauce made from piri piri chillies.
It's available in many supermarkets in hot and mild versions. It makes
a fantastic marinade for chicken or pork and can be added to soups
and stews to provide a bit of heat.

PREPARATION TIME: less than 20 minutes

COOKING TIME: 30–60 minutes

SERVES 4

150 g (5½ oz) brown rice

For the salsa:
1 tsp olive oil
½ red onion, peeled and finely chopped
2 cloves of garlic, peeled and crushed
4 mini sweet orange peppers or 1 orange pepper
10 cherry tomatoes
1 tsp red wine vinegar
2 tsp hot piri piri sauce
400 g (14 oz) tinned black-eye beans, drained and rinsed

1 Put the rice on to boil – this will take 35–40 minutes.

2 In the meantime, prepare the salsa. Heat the oil in a small pan and add the
red onion. Cook for 3–4 minutes before adding the garlic. Cut the pepper into
thin slices and add to the pan. Cut the larger cherry tomatoes in half, leaving
the smaller ones whole. Add to the pan along with the remaining ingredients.
Bring to the boil then simmer for 10 minutes.

3 When the rice is tender, drain and stir into the bean salsa.

$\mathcal{V}$ = suitable for vegetarians   ✕ = gluten free   ✕ = dairy free   = source of fibre

Dhal

Dhal is a lentil purée seasoned with curry spices. Tarka dhal is dhal made with red lentils but other pulses can be used, such as split yellow peas (channa dhal) and mung beans (moong dhal). This can be served as part of an Indian meal or on its own with boiled brown or basmati rice or wholemeal pitta bread.

PREPARATION TIME: less than 10 minutes

COOKING TIME: 30–60 minutes

SERVES 4

2 tsp vegetable oil
1 heaped tsp mustard seeds
1 onion, peeled and chopped
2 cloves of garlic, peeled and crushed
3-cm (1¼-in) piece of ginger, grated
250 g (9 oz) red lentils, rinsed and drained
½ tsp turmeric
½ tsp garam masala
Good pinch of salt
Small bunch of fresh coriander

157

1 Heat the oil in a frying pan and cover with a lid. Add the mustard seeds and cook over a medium-high heat until they start to pop, for approximately 5 minutes. Turn down the heat and add the onion. Cook for 5–6 minutes to soften without colouring. Add the garlic and ginger and cook for a further 2 minutes.

2 Stir in the red lentils and pour over 700 ml (1½ pints) boiling water. Bring to the boil and simmer, covered, for 15 minutes. After this time, add the turmeric and garam masala and cook for a further 10 minutes, until the lentils are completely tender. Add a little more water if necessary to achieve a porridge-like consistency.

3 When the lentils are soft, season well with salt and top with chopped coriander.

♥ = heart healthy   🍎 = counts towards 5-a-day   ✕ = lower fat

sweet
treats

Individual rhubarb crumbles

When making fruit crumble, you have a great opportunity to turn a treat dessert into a valuable source of nutrients. So instead of loading your fruit with sugar and making the topping with butter and white, processed flour, keep the sugar to a minimum and pack the topping with seeds, nuts and wholemeal flour.

PREPARATION TIME: less than 10 minutes

COOKING TIME: 30–60 minutes

SERVES 2

For the fruit filling:
2 stalks of rhubarb, sliced
1 tsp semolina
1 tsp fructose
¼ tsp ground ginger

For the topping:
50 g (2 oz) muesli
10 g (⅓ oz) wholemeal flour
25 g (1 oz) polyunsaturated
   margarine

160

1 Preheat the oven to 180° C (350° F/gas mark 4). Start by making the filling. Place the rhubarb into two small oven-proof dishes and stir in the semolina, fructose and ginger.

2 To make the topping, stir the muesli and flour together and rub in the margarine. Use to top the rhubarb. Bake for 25–30 minutes before serving with natural yoghurt or fromage frais.

𝒱 = suitable for vegetarians   ✕ = gluten free   ✕ = dairy free   = source of fibre

Baked pears with ginger

Pears are a surprisingly good source of fibre – one pear provides around four times the amount of fibre as a slice of white bread. Baking the pears in a scented syrup makes this a healthy and delicious treat.

PREPARATION TIME: less than 10 minutes + marinating time

COOKING TIME: less than 30 minutes

SERVES 2

2.5-cm (1-in) piece of ginger, peeled and cut into coins
2 star anise
1 tsp runny honey
2 pears, peeled

1 Place the ginger, along with the star anise, honey and 4 tablespoons of boiling water in an oven-proof dish which is just large enough to hold the fruit. Set aside to infuse for at least 1 hour.

2 Preheat the oven to 190° C (375° F/gas mark 5). Cut the pears in half lengthways and place them into the dish. Bake for 25 minutes until the pears are completely tender and serve, drizzling the syrup over the fruit.

161

 = heart healthy = counts towards 5-a-day = lower fat

Braised rhubarb with orange

Did you know that rhubarb is a vegetable, not a type of fruit? This is certainly reflected in its nutritional content – 100 g/3½ oz (about 4 stalks), has only 18 calories! Rhubarb usually needs a lot of sugar to balance its tartness but this recipe uses low GI fructose instead.

PREPARATION TIME: less than 10 minutes

COOKING TIME: less than 10 minutes

SERVES 4

4 stalks of rhubarb
Zest and juice of 1 orange
2 tsp fructose

1 Cut the rhubarb into 1-cm (½-in) pieces and place in a wide saucepan with the orange juice and zest, and fructose. Bring to the boil, then simmer, uncovered, for 10 minutes.

2 This rhubarb can be served over porridge, stirred into yoghurt, with langues de chat biscuits or stirred into a mix of Greek yoghurt and whipped cream for a special occasion dessert.

$\mathcal{V}$ = suitable for vegetarians   ✗ = gluten free   ✗ = dairy free   = source of fibre

Apricots with mascarpone cream

Dried apricots plump up beautifully on cooking, so poaching them in wine and serving with creamy mascarpone makes for a delicious dessert.

PREPARATION TIME: less than 10 minutes

COOKING TIME: less than 30 minutes

SERVES 4

For the apricots:
250 g (9 oz) ready-to-eat dried apricots
100 ml (3½ fl oz) white wine
1 tsp runny honey
Cinnamon stick

For the mascarpone cream:
125 g (4½ oz) mascarpone cheese
100 ml (3½ fl oz) reduced fat Greek
   yoghurt
100 ml (3½ fl oz) low-fat natural
   yoghurt
30 g (1 oz) walnuts, chopped

163

1 Start by preparing the apricots. Place the apricots in a small saucepan, pour over the wine and honey, and add the cinnamon stick, broken in two. Bring to the boil, then simmer gently for 30 minutes, until the apricots are plump and tender.

2 In the meantime, make the mascarpone cream by mixing the mascarpone, yoghurts and walnuts together. Serve the apricots in ramekins topped with mascarpone cream.

♥ = heart healthy   = counts towards 5-a-day   ✕ = lower fat

Pears with almond and chocolate

There's good news for chocolate-lovers everywhere – chocolate has a low GI value! The not-so-good news is that this low value comes courtesy of its high fat content so it's still a wise move to limit chocolate to an occasional, not an everyday, treat. When you do eat chocolate, it makes sense to choose one with the highest cocoa content you can find. This means that it will have a much more intense flavour and the higher cocoa content means that a little will satisfy any chocolate craving.

PREPARATION TIME: less than 10 minutes

COOKING TIME: less than 10 minutes

SERVES 2

30 g (1 oz) plain chocolate, at least 70% cocoa solids
100 ml (3½ fl oz) reduced fat Greek yoghurt
½ tsp almond extract
2 large pears, ripe but still firm
1 Tbsp melted butter

1 Chop the chocolate roughly so some pieces are about ½ cm (¼ in), others much finer, almost as if the chocolate had been grated.

2 Pour the yoghurt into a bowl and stir in most of the chocolate pieces and almond extract. Refrigerate until needed.

3 Peel the pears and cut them into quarters. Cut out the core and then lightly brush the cut sides with the melted butter. Preheat a griddle pan and place the pears in the centre of the pan. Cook, without moving for 3 minutes, then turn onto the other cut side and cook for a further 3 minutes.

4 Place the pears onto serving plates and top with the chocolate almond yoghurt, sprinkling with the reserved chocolate pieces.

$\mathcal{V}$ = suitable for vegetarians $\mathbb{X}$ = gluten free $\mathbb{X}$ = dairy free   = source of fibre

Strawberries with citrus mascarpone

As well as being a rich source of vitamin C, strawberries contain other powerful anti-oxidants called anthocyanins and anti-cancer compounds called ellagitannins. They also provide fibre, potassium, B vitamins, magnesium and copper. So enjoy this dessert knowing you're doing your body good!

PREPARATION TIME: less than 10 minutes + marinating time

COOKING TIME: none

SERVES 4

For the strawberries:
400 g (14 oz) strawberries
Juice of ½ lime
½ tsp fructose

165

For the citrus mascarpone:
125 g (4½ oz) mascarpone cheese
100 ml (3½ fl oz) reduced fat Greek yoghurt
Zest from ½ lime
1 Tbsp chopped fresh mint

1 Hull the strawberries and cut them into bite-sized pieces. Place in a bowl and stir in the lime juice and fructose. Set aside for 1 hour for the flavours to infuse.

2 In the meantime, combine the mascarpone, Greek yoghurt, lime zest and mint. Serve the strawberries topped with the citrus mascarpone.

 ♥ = heart healthy   = counts towards 5-a-day   = lower fat

Baked maple cream

Maple syrup is intensely sweet so only a little is needed to give sweetness and that unique flavour to this dessert. Since this dessert is so rich, it is definitely for special occasions only and portion sizes here are kept small. Serve with fresh berries.

PREPARATION TIME: less than 10 minutes
COOKING TIME: 30–60 minutes
SERVES 3

2 egg yolks
2 dsp maple syrup
100 ml (3½ fl oz) double cream
40 ml (1½ fl oz) milk
Raspberries, to serve

166

1 Preheat the oven to 190° C (375° F/gas mark 5). In a small bowl, whisk the egg yolks and maple syrup together until pale and frothy. In a small saucepan, heat the cream and milk without boiling. Pour the warm cream into the egg yolks, whisking all the time, then pour the mix into three ramekins.

2 Bake in a bain-marie for 35 minutes. Serve either warm or refrigerate overnight. Serve with raspberries.

V = suitable for vegetarians   X = gluten free   X = dairy free   = source of fibre

Poached nectarines

Baking fruit is the ideal way to get a step closer to your 5-a-day and it makes reaching the target for fruit and vegetable intake an absolute treat! Baking can soften up stubbornly hard fruit and it also evaporates off the alcohol, leaving only the flavour of the wine.

PREPARATION TIME: less than 10 minutes
COOKING TIME: less than 30 minutes
SERVES 2

2 ripe nectarines
2 Tbsp Marsala or Madeira
1 vanilla pod, cut open lengthways
Reduced fat Greek yoghurt, to serve

Preheat the oven to 190° C (375° F/gas mark 5). Cut the nectarines in half and place them in an oven-proof dish just large enough to hold them. Pour over the Marsala or Madeira, 2 tablespoons of boiling water and tuck in the vanilla pod. Bake for 25 minutes until the nectarines are completely tender. Serve with a dollop of Greek yoghurt.

167

♥ = heart healthy   🍎 = counts towards 5-a-day   ✕ = lower fat

Cherry trifle

This trifle is ideal for when you don't have much time on your hands! A lot of cakes actually have low GI values, Madeira cake included, since the fat content helps bring this down. So even though this is low GI, portions should still be kept small and it's not an everyday dessert!

$\mathcal{V}$ PREPARATION TIME: less than 30 minutes
COOKING TIME: less than 10 minutes
SERVES 8–10

For the cherries:
300 g (10½ oz) ripe cherries
2 Tbsp brandy
2 tsp fructose
½ tsp vanilla extract

2 Tbsp flaked almonds

For the custard mix:
125 g (4½ oz) mascarpone cheese
200 ml (7 fl oz) reduced fat
   ready-made custard
100 ml (3½ fl oz) reduced fat Greek yoghurt

1 small ready-made Madeira cake

1 Start by preparing the cherries. Stone the cherries and place them in a small pan with 60 ml (2 fl oz) water, the brandy, fructose and vanilla extract. Bring to the boil and simmer for 5–6 minutes, to soften the cherries and to allow the alcohol to evaporate off. Strain through a sieve, reserving the liquid, and set aside to cool.

2 Heat a small pan and dry-fry the almonds for around 6 minutes, until golden and aromatic. Set aside to cool.

3 To make the custard mix, combine the mascarpone, custard and Greek yoghurt in a bowl, beating well to soften the cheese.

4 Cut the Madeira cake into slices about 1 cm (½ in) thick and use to line a serving bowl. Drizzle over the liquid from the cherries, allowing the cake to soak it up before adding more. Spoon over the cherries, then top with the custard mix. Sprinkle with the flaked toasted almonds before serving.

$\mathcal{V}$ = suitable for vegetarians   ✕ = gluten free   ✕ = dairy free   ⫴ = source of fibre

Cosmopolitan jelly

The only missing ingredient in this jelly is the vodka! Cranberries, lime and orange combine in a fun dessert that's suitable for children as well as adults – and makes a great way to get kids towards their recommended five portions of fruit and vegetables per day.

PREPARATION TIME: less than 20 minutes
COOKING TIME: less than 10 minutes
SERVES 4

Juice of 1 lime
2 tsp fructose
Approximately 500 ml (18 fl oz) cranberry juice
1 sachet gelatine
1 orange
100 g (3½ oz) fresh cranberries

1 Squeeze the juice from the lime into a measuring jug, add the fructose and bring the volume up to 500 ml (18 fl oz) with cranberry juice. Pour this into a small saucepan, sprinkle over the gelatine and allow to soften for around 1 minute. Heat gently to allow the gelatine to dissolve completely, then remove from the heat.

2 Cut slices from either end of the orange so it will sit flat on a plate. Using a very sharp knife, cut off the peel, taking as much white pith as possible, then cut out the segments of orange flesh. Divide these, along with the cranberries, between four cocktail or other serving glasses. Pour over the cranberry juice and refrigerate overnight.

169

Fruit and yoghurt dessert

This dessert allows you to enjoy fruit even out of season. It requires overnight refrigeration, or at least for 4 hours, but if you're really pressed for time, leave out the gelatine step altogether and serve it as a fool instead. Try out the variations below, too!

PREPARATION TIME: less than 20 minutes
COOKING TIME: less than 10 minutes + chilling time
SERVES 4

200 g (7 oz) tinned fruit in juice
1 sachet of gelatine
2 Tbsp lemon or lime juice
1 Tbsp fructose
200 ml (7 fl oz) low-fat natural yoghurt
200 ml (7 fl oz) reduced fat Greek yoghurt

1 Strain the tinned fruit, reserving the juice. Pour the juice into a small pan and sprinkle over the gelatine. Allow it to soften for a minute or so, then heat gently, allowing the gelatine to dissolve completely. Set aside to cool.

2 Place the fruit, citrus juice and fructose into a bowl, stir and set aside for 10 minutes to allow the fructose to dissolve. In the meantime, combine the yoghurts in a large bowl and mix together using a hand-held whisk. Keeping the motor running, slowly pour in the just cool gelatine mixture and whisk to combine. Fold in the fruit and sugar mix, then spoon into serving glasses or ramekins and refrigerate overnight.

Dessert with raspberries and toasted oatmeal

Use lemon juice where citrus juice is given in the basic recipe and top each serving with 1 tablespoon of toasted pinhead oatmeal.

Dessert with pineapple and ginger

Use lime juice where citrus juice is given in the basic recipe and mix in 4 sliced pieces of preserved ginger while adding the gelatine. Top with a crumbled ginger nut biscuit just before serving.

V = suitable for vegetarians   X = gluten free   XX = dairy free   ░ = source of fibre

Cardamom-scented mango

Mango provides a vast array of nutrients, being a rich source of beta-carotene and providing fibre, magnesium, potassium, vitamins B and C, calcium and iron. This dessert is ideal after a rich or spicy Indian meal!

PREPARATION TIME: less than 10 minutes
COOKING TIME: none
SERVES 2–3

1 tsp fructose
4 cardamom pods, broken open
Juice and zest of 1 lime
1 mango, peeled, cut into long thin strips

1 Prepare a syrup by combining the fructose, cardamom, lime juice and zest with 100 ml (3½ fl oz) water in a small saucepan. Bring to the boil, then simmer for 10 minutes to reduce slightly in volume.

2 Arrange the mango pieces on a serving dish and pour over the syrup. Set aside to infuse for 1 hour before serving.

171

♥ = heart healthy   🍎 = counts towards 5-a-day   ✗ = lower fat

Rainbow fruit salad

Basing your diet on the colours of the rainbow is an easy way to ensure that you get a wide range of nutrients! So enjoy this rainbow fruit salad and be sure that you're boosting your health and well on your way to 5-a-day!

PREPARATION TIME: less than 10 minutes
COOKING TIME: none
SERVES 4

1 ruby grapefruit, halved
½ mango
50 g (2 oz) blueberries
1 kiwi fruit, sliced
½ small cantaloupe melon, cut into chunks
½ small galia melon, cut into chunks
2 Tbsp white rum

172

Remove the fruit segments from one half of the grapefruit and juice the other half. Arrange all the fruit pieces on a serving plate and drizzle over the rum and grapefruit juice.

𝒱 = suitable for vegetarians   ✕ = gluten free   ✕ = dairy free   = source of fibre

Pink fruit and nut cake

The tradition of using root vegetables to sweeten cakes and desserts actually goes back centuries, but carrot cake is the only example of this that most of us are familiar with. If you tell anyone this cake is sweetened with beetroot, they might put the slice back on the plate so tell them after they have enjoyed a slice! This is nice served warm, with a dollop of Greek yoghurt or lower fat crème fraîche.

PREPARATION TIME: less than 20 minutes
COOKING TIME: 1 hour or more
MAKES 8–10 slices

250 g (9 oz) wholemeal flour
2 heaped tsp baking powder
¼ tsp each cinnamon, allspice and ground ginger
75 g (2½ oz) caster sugar
200 g (7 oz) beetroot, peeled and grated
100 g (3½ oz) sultanas
50 g (2 oz) walnuts, chopped
100 ml (3½ fl oz) vegetable oil
1 ripe banana, mashed
3 eggs, separated
50–75 ml (2–2½ oz) milk
Greek yoghurt, to serve

173

1 Preheat the oven to 180° C (350° F/gas mark 4) and line a 20-cm (8-in) round cake tin.

2 Sieve the flour, baking powder and spices into a large bowl. Stir in the sugar. In a separate bowl, add the beetroot, sultanas, walnuts, oil, mashed banana and egg yolks. In yet another large bowl, whisk the egg whites to the stiff peak stage.

3 Stir the beetroot mix into the dry ingredients until combined. Add enough milk to make a dropping consistency. Gently fold in a heaped tablespoonful of egg white before folding in the rest and pour the batter into the lined tin. Place at the top of the oven and bake for about 1 hour, or until a skewer inserted in the centre comes out clean. Remove from the tin and allow to cool on a wire rack before cutting. Serve with a spoonful of Greek yoghurt.

♥ = heart healthy   🍎 = counts towards 5-a-day   ✗ = lower fat